《瑷珲海关历史档案辑要》编委会

主　编：石巍巍

副主编：魏　巍

编　辑：杜　晔　张　念　张丽娜　陈　岠

瑷珲海关
历史档案辑要

监管征税（上）

（第三卷）

黑龙江省档案馆　编译

社会科学文献出版社
SSAP
SOCIAL SCIENCES ACADEMIC PRESS (CHINA)

目录

专题一

征税办法

1. 为哈尔滨救济俄国饥民会救济物资免税放行之指令事

[A.—29]

No. 4 COMMRS.

Aigun No. 86,262

INSPECTORATE GENERAL OF CUSTOMS,

PEKING, 19th October, 1921.

Sir,

I append, for your information and guidance, copy of Shui-wu Ch'u despatch No.1599, from which you will see that you are to pass free of duty any shipments to Siberia of food, clothing, and other articles for relief purposes, with the exception of such grain, the export of which is prohibited by standing instructions, applied for by the Harbin Society for the Relief of Russian Famine Sufferers, if found in agreement with chihchao issued by the Harbin Commissioner of Foreign Affairs. You are to keep a record of articles passed for this Relief Society and forward a statement, with Chinese version in duplicate, thereof when the Society's relief work has come to an end.

The above shipments are to be entered in your Government Stores Return, this despatch being

quoted

The Commissioner of Customs,

A I G U N .

quoted as authority in the Remarks column.

I am,

Sir,

Your obedient Servant,

F. Aglen

Inspector General.

APPENDIX.

APPENDIX .

稅務處令第一五九九號　中華民國十年十月十四日

准外交部咨稱據哈爾濱交涉員呈稱據本埠救濟俄國飢民會會長函稱本會前曾在埠募賑所有辦事人員純是義務募得食品物件蓋影概係舊物如衣服皮鞋汗衫以及其他物品雖無市廛價值而俄國飢民勢所必需懇允免稅等情呈請轉咨核復示遵再該會募集物品為數若干尚難懸揣如奉核准免稅可否由職署繕發該會執照以便報關驗放仍行補報備查等因查該會募賑物品請予免稅暨該交涉員所擬給照辦法是否可行應咨行查照核辦見復等因前來查哈爾濱救濟俄國飢民會所募集之食品物件既係為賑濟俄國飢民之用事屬善舉應准免稅由哈爾濱交涉員繕發執照經過濱江愛琿等關查驗名色數目與執照相符即予放行倘有米穀等糧仍應禁止運出外國以符約章並將經照驗放之物品及數量彙案開單呈報本處備查除咨復并分行外相應令行總稅務司轉令各該關稅務司遵照辦理此令

柏春　同校
趙學謙

[A—29] 1 MAR 1922

No. 32 COMMRS.

Aigun No. 88,159

INSPECTORATE GENERAL OF CUSTOMS,

PEKING, 1st March, 1922.

Sir,

With reference to my despatch No. 4/86,262:

instructing you to pass free of duty any shipments to Siberia of food, clothing and other articles (with the exception of articles, of which export is prohibited by standing instructions) for relief purposes, applied for by the Harbin Society for the Relief of Russian Famine Sufferers (救济俄国饥民会), if found in agreement with Chihchao issued by the Harbin Commissioner of Foreign Affairs;

I append, for your information and guidance, copy of Shui-wu Ch'u despatch No. 263, from which you will see that you are to accord similar treatment to shipments to Siberia of relief articles applied for

Commissioner of Customs,

AIGUN.

for by the Chiu Chi O Min Hui (救濟俄民會) if covered by Chihchao issued by the Harbin Commissioner of Foreign Affairs.

I have to request you to act accordingly.

You are to keep a record of articles passed for this relief society and forward a statement, with Chinese version in duplicate, thereof when the Society's work has come to an end. These shipments are to be entered in your Government Stores Return.

I am,

Sir,

Your obedient Servant,

Inspector General.

I.G.despatch No. 32/88,159 to Aigun

A P P E N D I X.

稅務處令第二六三號 中華民國十一年二月二十四日

據吉林濱江道道尹兼哈爾濱交涉員張壽增快郵代電稱滿洲里站救濟俄民會於上年十二月間運往俄國災區小麥三火車經滿站稅關收取稅款九十四元四角三分外有募集舊衣履茶菸等物二百四十九普特經收稅款四十四元二角二分共一百三十八元六角五分該會援哈埠救濟會免稅辦法函請哈稅司轉飭發還經稅司復以應向哈交涉署請領相當執照等語即由該會函請敝署發給執照查哈埠救濟俄國飢民會報運糧貨悉請免稅均經電奉鈞署核示分別准駁轉飭遵照在案此次該會糧貨業已運出稅已完納復行援例請求返還稅款是否可行乞核示遵辦等因前來查滿站救濟俄民會所運小麥衣履茶菸等物業經車運出口既係專爲救濟俄國飢民之用應准特別通融免稅由滿站稅關將已收之稅鈔如數發還嗣後該會運出物品仍須領有哈埠交涉署相當執照方予免稅放行除電復外相應令行總稅務司轉令該關稅務司遵照辦理此令

由春 同校
趙學謙

致瑷珲关第 4/86262 号令　　　　　　海关总税务司署（北京）1921 年 10 月 19 日

尊敬的瑷珲关税务司：

为了便于贵署顺利执行，兹附中方税务处第 1599 号令，以供参考。据该令所示，若发现符合哈尔滨外交事务司签发的执照中所述情形，贵署应免税放行哈尔滨救济俄国饥民会申请运送到西伯利亚的食品、衣物及其他救济物资，但现行指示禁止出口的谷物等物品除外。贵署应记录救援会出关物品，并给税务处转发相应的缴税单，附中文版，一式两份，直至救援会救济工作结束。

应在政府退税表中登记上述装载货物，该令作为当局授权凭证填在“备注”栏中。

您忠诚的仆人

安格联（Francis Arthur Aglen）

海关总税务司

致瑷珲关第 32/88159 号令　　　　海关总税务司署（北京）1922 年 3 月 1 日

尊敬的瑷珲关税务司：

根据我签发的第 4/86262 号令：

"指示贵署若发现符合哈尔滨外交事务司签发的执照中所述情形，应免税放行哈尔滨救济俄国饥民会申请运送到西伯利亚的食品、衣物及其他救济物资（现行指示禁止出口的谷物等物品除外）。"

为了便于贵署顺利执行，兹附中方税务处第 263 号令，以供参考。据该令所示，如果救济俄国饥民会申请运送到西伯利亚的救济物资是在哈尔滨外交事务司颁发的执照所载范围之内，则按类似办法处理。

敬请遵照此令执行。

贵署应记录救济会出关物品，并给税务处转发相应的缴税单，附中文版，一式两份，直至救济会救济工作结束。请将这些物资登记在"官用物料报告表"中。

您忠诚的仆人

安格联（F. A. Aglen）

海关总税务司

2. 为呈报拟与中国银行签订税款代收合同事

21

I. G.

Aigun / Taheiho 14th January, 1922.

Sir,

1. With reference to your Despatch No. 15/87,200 and to my despatch No. 16 :

concerning a Separate Agreement with the Bank of China for the Collection and the Remittance of Revenue;

and to your telegram of 16th December :

instructing to continue to work under the Harbin Agreement pending further negotiations,

I have the honour to report that I resumed the discussions with the local Acting Manager of the Bank of China, and that having been informed by him that changes in the Harbin contract were being discussed, I enquired of the Harbin Commissioner about the extent and purport of such modifications.

2. In reply I received copy of Harbin Despatch No. 2568 / I. G., containing the proposed modifications to

The Inspector General of Customs,

PEKING

to the original Agreement.

3. In the meantime, deeming futile to discuss any longer with the local Branch of the Bank which, in the absence of the Manager, must refer every step to Changchun, I asked the Acting Manager whether he could get instructions to accept the same terms as would eventually be agreed upon between the Harbin Commissioner and the Harbin Branch of the Bank, and suggested that points in dispute be submitted to the Inspector General of Customs and the Head Office of the Bank in Peking, thereby avoiding useless delays.

4. The Acting Manager now informs me that he is instructed to follow the lead of the Harbin Office, and I have therefore the honour to submit, herewith enclosed, certain modifications to the proposed Agreement as drafted in my despatch No. 16. If the Agreement with this Office could be discussed at the same time as the Harbin Amended Agreement, there would be a gain in time and in uniformity.

I have followed the Harbin text very

closely,

closely, and, like the Harbin Commissioner, can see no objections to our cancelling the clause concerning interests on Revenue Balances, nor on leaving the Bank free to accept any local Bank Notes, provided they are responsible for the collection under the conditions stipulated in Article 7 of the Contract.

5. The Bank here contends that 1 % on Revenue Côllection is insufficient to meet expenses, and the difference of points of view cannot be settled locally; but the Bank could understand the moral advantage of its official status as Customs Bank, and be made to yield somewhat in return.

6. Concerning the rate of remittances, I think it would be a useless duplication of work if I were to discuss the quartorly rate, while the Harbin Commissioner does the same at his end. I therefore asked the Bank if they would agree to have the rates wired every quarter from Harbin, adding a fixed percentage for additional expenses between here and Harbin - there being

practically

practically no direct business between here and Shanghai. I suggest that 6 ‰ be added, this being the amount charged under the old Agreement for remittances from here to Harbin or Shanghai. Considering the expenses and risk in remitting from here to Harbin, this amount does not seem unreasonable, and the Acting Manager of the Bank agrees to my proposal. I left however the amount in blank on the revised draft of Article 3, as it may form matter for negotiations in connexion with the charges on collection.

7. I have besides provided for a fixed remittance fee of 6 ‰ from here to Harbin, as it may be expedient at times to remit money that way, but this clause is not essential, and may be deleted against other advantages. - Again, I made no mention of the currency of the Remittances, as dollars may be more convenient now, but changed conditions may render remittances in Taels advisable.

I have

I have the honour to be,

Sir,

Your obedient Servant,

Acting Commissioner.

Enclosure to Aigun despatch No. 21/I.G.

Proposed Amendments to Draft Agreement submitted in Aigun despatch No. 16.

Article 3. The Bank shall remit thatcollection at such times and in such manner as may be directed by the Commissioner. All remittances from Aigun/Taheiho to Shanghai shall be made by the Bank at a remittance fee equal to the one fixed quarterly between the Harbin Commissioner of Customs and the Harbin Branch of the Bank of China, plus %o.

In case money is to be remitted to Harbin, the remittance fee shall be 6 per mille.

No interest on Revenue collection balances will be paid by the Bank.

Article 7. The Bank undertakes to receive the duties, which are payable in Haikwan Taels, in big silver dollars (Peiyang, Yuan Shih K'ai and Hongkong) or in such local big silver dollar

三銀行所存稅款其滙解之期及手續均聽稅務司指令辦理其由愛琿（大黑河）滙滬之款滙費按照哈爾稅務司與哈埠中國銀行所規定每三月之行市每千元酌加　元（滙至哈爾濱滙費每千元六元）所有存之稅餉餘款概不計息

七銀行代收稅款以現大洋（如袁世凱像北洋及站人）或本地無折扣無限兑現之貨

dollar Bank Notes that are redeemable at their face value without restriction and in unlimited amount. The rate for Haikwan Taels vis-a-vis silver dollar and or local Bank Notes as defined above is fixed at Haikwan Taels 100.00 = $156.65. The Bank is responsible to the Commissioner for the actual amount of dollars collected at the above rate (i.e. in clean silver dollars or in local Bank Notes that are redeemable at their face value without restriction and in an unlimited amount).

幣核計關平銀兩每百兩定價按大洋一五六六五核算銀行允按以上定價現大洋或按無折扣無限兑現貨幣解交稅款

呈海关总税务司署 21 号文　　瑷珲关 / 大黑河 1922 年 1 月 14 日

尊敬的海关总税务司（北京）：

1. 根据海关总税务司署第 15/87200 号令及瑷珲关第 16 号呈：

“呈送为中国银行代收及汇寄税款事所拟之合同草本。”

及海关总税务司署 12 月 16 日电令：

“指示继续照哈尔滨关所签协议办理，以待进一步协商。”

兹报告，本署已重新开始与中国银行大黑河支行代理行长商讨此事，获悉对哈尔滨关所签协议之修改仍于商议之中。为此，本署已向哈尔滨关税务司询问修改的主要内容和范围。

2. 兹已收悉哈尔滨关关于拟议修改事项之呈文抄件（即哈尔滨关致海关总税务司署第 2568 号呈）。

3. 与此同时，由于中国银行大黑河支行行长不在本地，代理行长一切事宜皆需提请长春方面指示。如此一来，本署若继续与代理行长商讨，亦是毫无意义，遂已请其向上级请示接受哈尔滨关税务司与中国银行哈尔滨支行最终订立之合同条款，并建议将存有争议之处呈报海关总税务司及中国银行北京总行，以避免无谓之拖延。

4. 代理行长现已接到指示，将照哈尔滨分行之决定办理；有鉴于此，特此附上瑷珲关第 16 号呈所附合同之修改草本，希望可与哈尔滨关所签协议的修改之事一并商讨，以便节约时间，同时保证两份协议的一致性。

关于修改之事，本署已严格遵照哈尔滨关文本所列，且与哈尔滨关税务司一样，同意取消税款余额计息条款，允许中国银行接受其他当地银行所发行之纸币，唯须其遵照第七项条款负责收税事宜。

5. 大黑河支行代理行长表示，以所征税款之 1% 为酬劳费不足以满足各项开支，然此事亦无法于当地解决；但其亦深知作为海关银行所拥有之官方地位及道义优势，遂可为此略做让步。

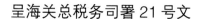

6. 至于汇款至上海的汇费，兹以为，哈尔滨关税务司既已在商讨季度之数额，本署再重复此举毫无意义，且瑷珲（大黑河）与上海几乎无直接经济往来，故已向大黑河支行提议由哈尔滨关按季以电报通知汇费数额，本地仅须于此数之上增加固定比例费用即可。对此，兹提议照哈尔滨关所定之季度汇费每千元增加六元，此前合同草本中，由瑷珲（大黑河）汇至哈尔滨之汇款汇费即为每千元六元，而且考虑到汇款所需费用，所担风险，该比例应属

合理，大黑河支行代理行长对此亦表示赞同。然因此费用与银行收税酬劳金有关，或须再议，故本署并未于附件第三项条款中填写确切数额。

7. 鉴于有时需将税款汇至哈尔滨，本署拟将由瑷珲（大黑河）汇至哈尔滨之汇费定为千分之六，当然，此项条款并非十分紧要，若与其他条款有所冲突，亦可删除。本署并未于修改草本中提及汇款货币种类，以当前情况来看，银圆或更为方便，但若情况有变，亦可使用海关两。

您忠诚的仆人

包安济（G. Boezi）

署理税务司

拟议对瑷珲关第16号呈所附合同之修改

三、银行所存税款，其汇解之期及手续均听税务司指令办理；其由瑷珲（大黑河）汇沪之款，汇费按照哈尔滨关税务司与中国银行哈尔滨支行所规定每三月之行市每千元酌加______元，汇至哈尔滨汇费千分之六；所有存之税饷余款概不计息。

七、银行代收税款以现大洋（即现银圆），如北洋、袁世凯像及站人（香港银圆），或本地无折扣无限兑现之货币核计。海关两每百两定价按大洋一百五十六元六角五分核算。银行允按以上定价现大洋或按无折扣无限兑现货币解交税款。

3. 为告知在中国使用过且在复出口到国外时仍能识别为洋货的货物可免税复出口但不予以退税事

31

I. G. Aigun / Taheiho 25th February, 1922.

Sir,

I have the honour to report that a Chinese gentleman interested in the overland Motor traffic to Tsitsihar imported some time ago from Blagovestchensk a second-hand Talbot Motor Car, valued at Hk. Tls. 1,000. The Motor Car is borrowed from a Russian in Siberia; it is now run as a commercial venture between Taheiho and Tsitsihar, and it is intended for re-exportation to Blagovestchensk in the Spring. The importer paid Duty and Famine Relief Surtax, but asked if I could see my way of refunding the duty (Hk. Tls. 50.000) when the car is sent back to the owner in Blagovestchensk. I said the issue was rather uncertain, as the car could not be said to be "in the original conditions" on re-exportation. However, on his insisting, I promised to refer the question to your decision.

I

The Inspector General of Customs,

PEKING.

I now have the honour to enquire whether I may issue drawbacks, on re-exportation abroad, to foreign goods which, although identifiable, have been put to use in China; or allow such goods to be imported on deposit. In the past, pianos belonging to ships hibernating here have thus been admitted on deposit: the pianos are used in some hotels or restaurants during the winter, and put again on board steamer at the opening of the navigation. The same treatment is granted kynematograph films imported by theatres and hotels, not by travelling showmen.

I have the honour to be,

Sir,

Your obedient Servant,

G. Bocchi

Acting Commissioner.

No. 34 Commrs.

Aigun No. 88,539

INSPECTORATE GENERAL OF CUSTOMS,

PEKING, 22nd March, 1922.

SIR,

I am directed by the Inspector General to acknowledge receipt of your Despatch No. 31 :

enquiring if you may issue drawbacks, on re-exportation abroad, to foreign goods which, although identifiable, have been put to use in China;

and, in reply, to say that if the goods are identifiable as foreign you may allow re-export free of duty, but drawback is not to be issued.

I am,

Sir,

Your obedient Servant,

Cecil A. V. Bowra,

Chief Secretary.

The Commissioner of Customs,

A I G U N.

呈海关总税务司署 31 号文　　　　瑷珲关 / 大黑河 1922 年 2 月 25 日

尊敬的海关总税务司（北京）：

兹汇报，一名在大黑河与齐齐哈尔两地经营汽车运输生意的华籍男子，日前从西伯利亚一名俄籍男子手中租借了一辆二手塔伯特汽车，并于布拉戈维申斯克（Blagovestchensk[①]）将之运入大黑河，该汽车价值 1000 海关两。目前该汽车用于接揽大黑河与齐齐哈尔两地之间的运输生意，计划于今年春季复出口至布拉戈维申斯克。

上述华籍男子在进口汽车时已完纳关税和附征赈捐，现欲知该汽车复出口至布拉戈维申斯克时，能否获得退税（5000 海关两）。本署已向其说明，以该汽车目前之状况来看，难以归为"原装"复出口之货物，因此能否退税尚无法确定。然无奈其一再坚持，本署只得应允向贵署呈请指示。

特此请示，对于此等已于中国投入使用之洋货（可证实来源），复出口时能否退税，或者是否可按进口暂存货物处理。此前，有些轮船于大黑河过冬时，船上的钢琴便获准按照暂存货物办理，停留期间可供一些酒店或餐馆借用，待航运季开始后，再搬回轮船。影院及酒店亦可使用此法进口电影胶片，但流动放映商不得如此。

您忠诚的仆人

包安济（G. Boezi）

瑷珲关署理税务司

① 即海兰泡。

致瑷珲关第 34/88539 号令　　　　海关总税务司署（北京）1922 年 3 月 22 日

尊敬的瑷珲关税务司：

第 31 号呈收悉：

“询问如果可证明是洋货且已在中国使用的货物，在复出口到国外时是否予以退税。”

奉总税务司命令，现批复如下：如果货物可识别为洋货，贵署可予以免税复出口，但不可再退税。

您忠诚的仆人

包罗（C. A. V. Bowra）

总务科税务司

4. 为拟对土货征收复进口半税事

Aigun / Taheiho 3rd April, 1922.

Sir,

1. In my despatch No. 32, § 13, I had the honour to recommend that the question of levying Coast Trade Duty be considered in conjunction with the solution of the Liangchiat'un question, and in the proposed New Regulations submitted in my despatch No. 37, and more particularly in Articles 21 and 22, levy of Coast Trade Duty is anticipated.

2. In this connection I have the honour to report that, when this District was opened, the levy of Coast Trade Duty was not enforced; but, while the Sungari Regulations issued in 1910 make no mention of this particular Duty, the Aigun Customs Provisional Regulations issued in July 1909 specifically

Inspector General of Customs,

PEKING.

specifically state that it is leviable (Articles 2, 7, 9 and 11), with a clause to Article 7, which says that this Duty would "for the present only be "levied by the Aigun Customs if the goods are "destined for places outside the 100 li zone".

3. Nobody, of course, ever declared goods for places outside the 100 li zone, and in practice the Duty was never collected; but even when the duty free zone was abolished in 1914, the levy of Coast Trade Duty was not enforced, presumably due to the opposition of the Russian Authorities, and because Trade was still insufficiently developed.

4. Conditions, however, have changed since; the Trade has grown, as evidenced by the increase in Value and Revenue in the last ten or twelve years - and our Returns do not show the huge profits made by the Gold Miners, the smugglers and the financial parasites in this District. Fortunes are being made and squandered, and a light burden would certainly not kill the Trade.

5. There has been a depression one year ago, following on the unprecedented boom of 1918 - 1920,

and

and it may be questioned whether it is advisable to enforce the levy of this Duty at once, or to wait for a fuller recovery from the setback of one year ago; on this point the opinion of the Harbin Commissioner will be most valuable, as he is in a better position to judge in advance, from the Commercial Centre of North Manchuria; he is also directly concerned because, if Aigun/Taheiho is to tax Native Goods imported from the Sungari, Harbin is similarly to levy Coast Trade Duty on Native Goods imported from Aigun/Taheiho.

6. However, the principle that Coast Trade Duty is leviable had better be asserted at once; already, in compliance with the instructions of your despatch No. 14/87,199, § 1, Postal Parcels are treated in accordance with Shanghai practice, and charged Coast Trade Duty when collectable. I therefore beg to recommend that, if you consider that levy is to be postponed until trade prospects look brighter, the Merchants be made anyhow to pledge themselves to raise no opposition, whenever you decide that Levy is to be started - in exchange for concessions in the matter of taxation of overland Traffic.

7. In

7. In drafting the New Regulations, I added a Note to Articles 21 and 22, exempting for the present from Coast Trade Duty Goods moved along the Amur. For the time being levy, in my opinion, is out of question, there being only one Port on the Amur; but even if, in a near future, Taheiho be declared an open Port, or we open new Stations, Goods moved within the District should pay one full duty only - in order not to discourage the growing Inter-District traffic.

8. I estimate the collection at 20,000 or 25,000 Hk. Tls.; in 1921 the value of Native Imports by River amounted to Hk. Tls. 1,846,000, out of which 70 %, or about Hk. Tls. 1,290,000 from the Sungari - duty would not have been inferior to my figures.

Copy of this despatch is sent to the Harbin Commissioner.

I have the honour to be,

Sir,

Your obedient Servant

G. Boezi

Acting Commissioner.

928.

9.

Harbin 21st April, 1922.

SIR,

With reference to Aigun Despatch No. 38 to the Inspector General, copy of which was supplied to this Office :

concerning a proposal to enforce the levy of Coast Trade duty on native goods moved between Aigun/Taheiho and the Sungari ports :

I beg to report that while the revision of the Aigun Customs Provisional Regulations, preconised in my Despatches Nos. 2348, 2379 and 2394 of 1920 and now taken in hand by the Aigun Commissioner, is a very necessary measure, and while our right to collect Coast Trade duty on native goods moved between the Amur Port (Aigun/Taheiho) and the Sungari Ports (Lahasusu, Sansing and Harbin) should be reiterated in the revised regulations, yet the

actual

The Inspector General of Customs,

PEKING.

actual enforcement of the levy of Coast Trade duty should, in my opinion, be postponed until trade conditions in the Amur and Sungari districts have materially improved. New tax offices are springing up like mushrooms in the Northern Manchurian Provinces and trade is so overburdened with taxes that the levy of another duty by the Maritime Customs, even if it did add some Taels 20,000,000 to the revenue, is not advisable at this stage. Postponement is also recommended in view of the remarks made by the Inspector General in his Despatch No. 2809/88,114 to this office that "a movement is in progress that must sooner or later, probably sooner, lead to the abolition of Export and Coast Trade duties and it is not desirable that we should inaugurate a system leading in the opposite direction".

A copy of this Despatch is being sent to the Aigun Commissioner.

I have the honour to be,

Sir,

Your obedient Servant,

(Signed) R. C. L. d'Anjou.

Commissioner.

True Copy:-

C H Bencraft [signature]

2nd Assistant A:

呈海关总税务司署38号文　　　　瑷珲关/大黑河1922年4月3日

尊敬的海关总税务司（北京）：

1. 本署曾于瑷珲关第32号呈（第13项）提出梁家屯分卡解决方案时，建议征收土货复进口半税，并于瑷珲关第37号呈提交的拟议新章程（第21及22条）中对该税之征收事宜有所提及。

2. 然而，自瑷珲关区开埠以来，从未征收过土货复进口半税，1910年颁布之《松花江行船章程》中亦未提及此税，但1909年7月颁布之《瑷珲分关试办章程》（第2、7、9及11条）中已列明此税可征，其中第7条指明“凡货物拟运至百里免税区以外各地者，目前可由瑷珲关征收土货复进口半税”。

3. 不过，商人自然不会申报货物运往百里免税区以外各地，因此瑷珲关实际上也从未征收过此税；而且1914年百里免税区被废除后，或因俄国政府之反对，加之此地贸易仍不繁荣，征收土货复进口半税之事一直未能实现。

4. 然时移世易，在过去的10至12年间，物价上涨、税收增加，足以证明贸易有增长之态，而且瑷珲关的收益报表中还不包括本地金矿矿主、走私商贩及各路不劳而获之人所获之巨大利润，不过此等钱财最终还是被挥霍掉，对贸易并未造成太大影响。

5.1918年至1920年贸易空前繁荣，但1921年贸易显现不景气之现象，故此税是否应立即征收，或是待至贸易完全恢复后再行征收，实难决策；对此，哈尔滨关税务司身处北满洲贸易中心，应该可以更好地做出预判，所给意见亦更具价值；而且若瑷珲口岸和大黑河口岸对自松花江进口之土货征税，哈尔滨关亦可对自瑷珲或大黑河运入松花江之土货征收复进口半税。

6. 当然，土货复进口半税的征收办法还是早定为宜；目前，瑷珲关已照海关总税务司署第14/87199号令指示，依江海关之惯例办理邮政包裹征税事宜，凡符合条件者，概征收复进口半税。若贵署认为应于贸易前景更为明朗时再征此税，兹建议，无论何时开始征税，均应保证商人不会提出异议，为此，海关或可在对陆路运输征税事宜上做出妥协。

7. 本署于拟议新章程的第21与22条项下备注说明，暂不对黑龙江沿岸往来运输货物征收复进口半税，主要是考虑到黑龙江沿线目前仅有一个通商口岸，是否应施行此项征税，仍有疑虑。而且兹认为，即便将来增设分卡，为鼓励各区间的货物运输，亦应对瑷珲关区内运输之货物仅征一次正税。

8. 若对经松花江进口之土货征收复进口半税，预计可征得20000至25000海关两；

1921 年经水运进口之土货的价值合计 1846000 海关两，其中 70%，约 1290000 海关两之货物皆为自松花江进口，因此实际之数不会低于本署估算数额。

此抄件已发送至哈尔滨关税务司。

您忠诚的仆人
包安济（G. Boezi）
瑷珲关署理税务司

呈海关总税务司署2628号文　　　　　　　　　　哈尔滨关1922年4月21日

尊敬的海关总税务司（北京）：

根据瑷珲关致海关总税务司署第38号呈（抄件已发送至哈尔滨关）：

“建议对瑷珲/大黑河与松花江沿岸各地间往来之土货征收复进口半税。”

兹认为，瑷珲关税务司目前着手办理瑷珲关《瑷珲分关试办章程》修订之事十分必要，本署早于1920年哈尔滨关第2348号、2379号及2394号呈中有所说明，对黑龙江沿线口岸（瑷珲/大黑河）与松花江沿岸各口（拉哈苏苏、三姓及哈尔滨）往来之土货征收复进口半税之事亦应载于修订章程之中，但实际征收应待黑龙江与松花江地区的贸易状况发生实质性改善后再行开展。

而且目前，税捐局办事处于北满洲如雨后春笋般涌现，商人税负过重，恐难以再承担海关加征任何关税，尽管海关税收可因此而增加约20000.00海关两，但于此阶段征收此种关税实非明智之举。此外，海关总税务司已于致哈尔滨关第2809/88114号令中指示“依目前形势来看，出口税及复进口半税迟早会被废除，此时不宜反其道而行之”。基于此，亦建议推迟土货复进口半税征收一事。

此抄件已发送至瑷珲关税务司。

您忠诚的仆人

（签字）覃书（R. C. L. d'Anjou）

哈尔滨关税务司

此抄件内容真实有效，特此证明：

录事：周骊（C. H. B. Joly）二等帮办前班

5. 为俄中央联社远东分社要求其于1921年复出口至布拉戈维申斯克之货物征税款悉数退还事

2 Enclosures.

159. TRANS-FRONTIER TRADE: $58,181.97 claimed by Dalcentrosoyus on cargo re-exported to Blagovestchensk in 1921; claim rejected; further demands likely if present claim is entertained; case stated in full.

I.G.

Aigun 7th. April, 1924.

Replied to in No. 17[illegible]

Sir,

1\. The " All-Russian Central Union of " " Consumers' Societies " (Dalcentrosoyus) have claimed refund of duties amounting to $58,181.97 collected by this office on cargo imported into Taheiho overland *via* Tsitsihar and Liangchiat'un during November and December, 1920, and the first four months of 1921, and re-exported to Blagovestchensk during the first six months of 1921. Application for Drawback was not made at the time when the cargo was sent to Blagovestchensk, and there is consequently nothing to show that this cargo, when re-exported, was entitled to drawback privilege. There is only proof of the allegation that this cargo, when re-exported, was released without payment of duty. The claim has been rejected, but I have informed the manager of the " All-Russian Central Union of " " Consumers' Societies " that the case is being referred to you.

2.

The Inspector General of Customs,

Peking.

Entered in Card-Index.

2. I will preface any further remarks about this claim for $58,181.97 (received by letter of 27th. February, 1924) with a recital of what took place in October, 1923, when the " All-Russian " " Central Union of Consumers' Societies " applied for refund of ~~$23,187.40~~ which they maintained had been over-collected by this office during November and December, 1920, and the first six months of 1921 on various consignments of winter clothing, boots, etc., (military equipment) imported overland <u>via</u> Tsitsihar and Liangchiat'un and re-exported to Blagovestchensk during the period from 1st. January to 30th. June, 1921. The claim was based on the ground that this office, for duty assessment purposes, had placed too high a value on the cargo, and it was sought to support this view by means of a " Declaration " (Letter No. 7445 of the 16th. of August, 1923) received from the Harbin branch of the " All-Russian Central Union of " " Consumers' Societies ." There accompanied this " Declaration " :-

(1)

(1) 21 Custom House Receipts ;

(2) Statement of Reckoning ;

(3) 24 Specifications ;

(4) 24 Copies of Invoices ;

(5) Copy of Information of the Chinese Commercial Union No. 556 dated 28th. April, 1922 ; and

(6) Letter of the Russo-Belgian Company dated April, 17th.,1923, regarding the right of Centrosoyus to receive the overcharge made (with English translation):

I enclose, for inspection and return, 22 Customs Duty Receipts. There were 21 Receipts enclosed in the Union's letter of 17th. September,1923, (asking for a refund of $23,187.40), but 22 Receipts were subsequently received together with the Union's letter of 27th. February, 1924 (asking for a refund of $58,181.97). I append :-

(a) Copy of (2) Statement of Reckoning - an English Document ;

(b) Copy of (5) Copy of Information of the Chinese Commercial Union No. 556 dated 28th. April, 1922 - a Russian Document to which is appended a translation made in this office ; and

(c) Copy of (6) Letter of the Russo-Belgian Company dated April, 17th., 1923, regarding the right of Centrosoyus to receive the overcharge made - a Russian document to which is appended a translation made by Centrosoyus:

The 24 Specifications and 24 Copies of Invoices have been returned.

3.

3. This matter was gone into carefully by this office and among the material points advanced by the Acting Tidesurveyor were the following:-

(1) The difference in price between Cotton Wadded Suits and Cotton Wadded Uniforms;

(2) The difference between the prices ruling in 1922 and 1920 and 1921; and

(3) The difference in the market prices of all kinds of goods at Harbin and Taheiho, especially in the winter months when everything has to be brought into this port overland at considerable expense.

Further, it may be noted :-

(1) That the Union regard the invoice value as the value on which duty should have been collected and that they disregard the fact that various charges have to be added;

(2) That taking the invoice value as a basis for duty collection it is found that the amount of duty said to have been over-collected is correctly given in 11 only of the 21 cases;

(3) That in some cases incomplete or wrong bills were attached to the Duty Receipts;

(4) That in the case of Duty Receipt No. 3651 the bills attached were not only incomplete, but the Chinese applications handed in at this office were not in agreement with the English applications on file;

(5) That in 3 cases surtax has been mixed up with duty;

(6) That practically the whole of the cargo was declared at this office by Kung Chi Chan, Customs Broker, and that while it is agreed that the values declared were lower than the

the Customs values, it is not agreed that the latter were too high;

(7) That there are neither marks nor numbers on the applications; that there is nothing to show that there were marks and numbers on the original packages; and that if cargo, declared by the Union as being the original cargo, should be brought to the Shed for re-examination this office would not agree that such cargo was the same as that which had previously passed through its hands; and

(8) That the sum total, as per Statement of Reckoning, of duty said to have been over-charged amounts to $22,217.41 whereas the amount claimed by the Union is $23,187.40.

4. In my written reply to the Union I made no attempt at anything approaching a reasoned argument because I thought it prudent to say as little as possible. A representative who was sent to call for the money was given to understand that the policy upon which our examination of cargo rested was that of direct challenge to anything in the nature of adverse criticism; that re-consideration of Customs Values necessitated re-examination of the cargo concerned; and that this office could not agree in October, 1923, to change values which had been accepted as correct in December, 1920, and January, 1921. He was told that the accounts

for

for 1920 and 1921 were closed and that the request could not be entertained. My attitude in this case has been, so to speak, to laugh the plaintiff out of court and I submit that an opinion arrived at by our examiners at the end of 1920 should not be subject to criticism or capable of controversy in October, 1923. It forms no part of our duty to invite a merchant to apply for a Drawback and if he should decide not to apply, it seems to me that the choice should be considered as having been made for good. I venture the opinion that those who now seek to change the rules to their own advantage should be required to recognise the " fait accompli " and that they should not be allowed to upset it.

5. I had hoped that this matter would be allowed to end here, but this has not been the case and the original claim for $23,187.40 has now reached the formidable total of $58,181.97. [...ndix 8.] It is no longer a Drawback for duties said to have been erroneously collected as a result of

over-valuation

over-valuation of the cargo that is now applied for. What is demanded by the " All-Russian Central " Union of Consumers' Societies " in their letter of the 27th. of February, 1924, is the refund of all duties collected by this office on the cargo in question and the Union evidently expect us to meet their demand notwithstanding the unfortunate circumstance that delay in submitting their claim makes it impossible for them to prove that thay are entitled to consideration. The Union profess to believe that a merchant who is entitled to a Drawback may apply for it whenever it suits his convenience to do so, and that the special interest of a Custom House in such a case is a matter of unimportant consideration. Their attitude seems to be : " Your office has accepted under " " Treaty the obligation to issue Drawbacks; we " " look to you to carry out that obligation." Here we have, stripped of all frills and coverings, the

dix 9. kernel of the question raised. I have objected that application for Drawback three years after

cargo

cargo has been re-exported infringes the principle that a Custom House which is asked to find the money has a right to demand abundant proof that the application is in order, and that omission to apply for Drawback, whatever the motive, presupposes that the cargo was not entitled to it - that it has been re-packed and is to all intents and purposes cargo which has not previously been sent for examination. A Custom House has always to be on guard against unscrupulous people who specialise in swindling the revenue and the refund of money under conditions now reported would involve a very considerable risk.

6. The " All-Russian Central Union of " " Consumers' Societies " in their letter of the 27th. February, 1924, lay stress on the following points :-

(1) That the Aigun Commercial Treaty of 1886 accords the privilege of duty free treatment to foreign goods and native goods of foreign type sent from China to Russia;

(2) That an Additional Agreement signed at Peking in 1914 by the Inspector General of Customs and the Russian Minister

Minister gave cover to a Duty Free List; that the Harbin Office recognised this List, and that since the Agreement was still in force when the cargo was re-exported to Russia it follows that the Aigun Office, at that time a branch office of the Harbin Customs, much also recognise it;

(3) That the time limit of 3 years allowed for refund of duty had not expired when the application for Drawback was received at the Aigun Office;

(4) That the Harbin Office regards an entry made on a Duty Receipt by a Customs Officer to the effect that cargo has been re-exported as sufficient proof that the cargo in question is entitled to Drawback; and

(5) That at the time when the Aigun Custom House was opened the public was notified that foreign cargo and native cargo of foreign type exported overland to Russia via Tsitsihar would be passed free of duty:

I venture to make the following comments :-

(1) It is assumed that the Union intended to refer to the Treaty of St. Petersburg of 1881 and in this connection it should be noted that export duty was not collected on the cargo at time of re-exportation. What has happened is that this office, at a time when it is no longer in a position to exercise the right of examination, has declined to pay over the sum of $58,181.97 without check or question because those who claim this sum are not able to prove that they are entitled to receive it. There is nothing to show that the cargo, at time of re-exportation, was in the same condition as that in which it arrived, and owing to the absence of marks and numbers it is very doubtful whether this could have been proved at the time when shipment was made to Blagovestchensk. It is reasonable to suppose that the foreign goods were passed free, on re-exportation, because the examiner was satisfied that they were foreign and that no export duty was collected on the native goods because they were of foreign

foreign style and in the Duty Free List. It is held that the real matter at issue is the question whether the cargo sent to Blagovestchensk was the same cargo as that which paid import duty on arrival at Taheiho. This material point is now no longer capable of proof, and it is therefore submitted that the question of Drawback does not arise;

(2) Here again the question of Drawback does not seem to arise owing to the impossibility of identifying the cargo. It is noticed that on the majority of the import applications there is no remark to the effect that the native goods were of foreig style;

(3) The rule that foreign cargo, which fulfills certain necessary conditions, may be re-exported against refund of duty within a period of three years from date of arrival in port, can not be taken to mean that a merchant who neglects to apply for a Drawback when his cargo is re-exported can claim the right to receive one, if it should suit his convenience so to apply, some 2 or 3 years after his cargo has left the port. It may sometimes happen that foreign cargo for which no Drawback is applied is passed, on re-exportation, without careful examination just because it is foreign and consequently free of duty. On the other hand, foreign cargo for which Drawback is required is very strictly examined and we regard marks and numbers as an essential check. This is the security of a long-established custom and we should not allow ourselves to be forced to compromise and dilute our principles;

(4) Remarks entered by this office on Duty Receipts are intended to call attention to the fact that the cargo covered by the Duty Receipt, or some portion of it, has been re-exported and that care is to be taken to see that no further application is made in this connection. These remarks are not meant to certify that cargo re-exported is in agreement as regards packing, marks and numbers with the cargo originally imported -that it is entitled to Drawback;

(5)

(5) The native goods were passed free when sent from Taheiho to Blagovestchensk because the movement was considered as being in the nature of direct traffic between China and Russia. These same goods, on arrival at Taheiho overland via Tsitsihar and Liangchiat'un, were required to pay import duty: (1) because the movement was not regarded as being in the nature of direct traffic between China and Russia and (2) because the cargo on arrival at this port was not declared as being destined for Blagovestchensk. As regards the foreign goods, import duty was levied because they were not declared as being intended for re-exportation to Russia. They were passed free when sent to Russia (Blagovestchensk) because we were satisfied that they were of foreign origin. Both the foreign and native goods were stored for some time at Taheiho outside Customs control.

7. It is just possible that the " All-Russian " " Central Union of Consumers' Societies " may pretend that the rejection of their application for Drawback indicates a deviation from usual office practice, but that this is not the case can be verified without much difficulty. Take, for instance, the following two examples :-

(1) In December, 1921, E.S.Sidortchook, ex-Tidewaiter, applied for a Drawback on foreign cargo imported by him in July, 1920, and re-exported to Blagovestchensk in September, 1920. His application was refused:(1) because he had omitted to apply at time of re-exportation; and (2) because the absence of marks and numbers made it impossible for him to establish full connection between the cargo originally imported and that subsequently re-exported:

(2)

(2) On the 11th. February, 1924, Kung Chi Chan, Customs Broker, imported overland *via* Tsitsihar and Liangchiat'un 4 packages of rubber tyres and 4 packages of steel springs for a motor car and forthwith declared his intention to re-export these 8 packages to Blagovestchensk. This office took a deposit of $35 to cover import duty leviable and lead seals were affixed to the 8 packages. On the 19th. February, 1924, when application was made for Drawback and permission to re-export, it was found that the 8 packages had been opened, the seals removed, and the tyres and springs fitted to the car. This office declined to grant Drawback on the ground that it was no longer in a position to identify the cargo and import duty was brought to account:

I venture the opinion that the above two cases support the argument that before a Drawback is issued this office exercises reasonable circumspection.

8. The present dispute has in reality a very wide range and if the superficial evidence of a number of Customs Duty Receipts - documents which prove that certain cargo, when re-exported, was released without further payment of duty, but do not prove that the cargo left China in its original condition - is to be the deciding factor, and the Union's application is granted, the effect will be much greater than we can measure in advance. The problem raised goes far beyond the issue as to

whether

whether or not a large sum of money, to which the applicants might, or might not, have been morally and equitably entitled in 1920 and 1921, should be handed over unconditionally to the party immediately concerned in 1924, when by reason of the time which has elapsed since the cargo was re-exported any opinion as to whether it was really entitled to Drawback privilege must be to a very great extent a matter of pure guesswork. The question really raised is whether or not, in the case of re-exports, the unproved assertion of any member of the public is to be accepted by us in lieu of definite proof. A claim of the kind made by the Union, if unchallenged, would constitute an intolerable precedent and so far as this port is concerned a more embarrassing situation could hardly arise because a disproportionate amount only of the duty collected on cargo imported and subsequently re-exported to Blagovestchensk, is refunded by means of Drawbacks. The comparatively large revenue collected during 1918 (Hk.Tls. 161,646),

1919

1919 (Hk.Tls. 128,893), and 1920 (Hk.Tls. 188,526) was almost entirely due to the false prosperity of the war period when, owing to the closing of the Trans-Siberian Railway to goods other than war materials, the importance of Taheiho as a distributing centre increased by leaps and bounds and everything it was possible for this port to send to Blagovestchensk found a ready market. By reference to our statistics it is easy to point to the increase in the value of re-exports to Russia during these years and to see that they are not on a pre-war scale. Here are the statistics -

Value of Re-exports to Russia 1915 - 1922.

1915:	Hk.Tls.	358,153	1919:	Hk.Tls.	2,212,525
1916:	,,	251,874	1920:	,,	3,582,686
1917:	,,	1,497,190	1921:	,,	1,484,682
1918:	,,	2,587,930	1922:	,,	1,126,507

These figures disclose the fact that the increase of so large a percentage in the value of imports during the war period - these rose from Hk.Tls. 3,044,839 in 1915 to Hk.Tls. 7,446,438 in 1918, Hk.Tls. 7,151,682 in 1919, and Hk.Tls. 7,042,905 in

1920

1920 - was not needed for local consumption, but that most of the stocks accumulated in such comparatively large quantities were sent to Blagovestchensk which was to a great extent dependent upon this market for its supplies. There are several merchants here who have in their possession Duty Receipts covering cargo imported and subsequently re-exported by them to Russia and I hear that they are waiting to pour their claims into this office. Refusal to depart from a rigid insistence that applications for Drawbacks must be made at time of re-exportation will act as a wholesome deterrent to these potential claimants; surrender to the Union's demand, on the other hand, will be likely to set innumerable claims in motion and cause endless confusion and mischief.

9. It is possible that the " All-Russian " " Central Union of Consumers' Societies ", a Government trading concern, may take up this case with a determination to see the thing through and that in due course dissatisfaction experienced locally

may

may swell into a considerable protest at Peking. If, as is apparently the case, the authorities at Blagovestchensk are fairly gravelled for lack of funds, big influence may be used behind the scenes to enforce the claim. I submit, however, that in this matter Reason is strongly on our side and that in the circumstances the claim advanced is unjustified and unjustifiable. The manager of Dalcentrosoyus should understand that a Custom House works by certain rules and that we have as much right to take fundamental and vital revenue interests clearly and fully into account as he has, after three years' procrastination, to display such scrupulous care for the welfare of his company. If he is a practical man he should appreciate that point of view perfectly well and recognise that a claim such as he presents must fall to the ground in default of definite proof that it is a just one.

10. I should add that there is living at Taheiho a Mr. E. S. Sidortchook, an ex-Tidewaiter, and

and that it is generally supposed that the case against this office has been to a great extent prepared and probably inspired by this man. In my opinion it is not fanciful to think that Mr. Sidortchook is working against us on a commission basis and that he has been promised a share of the profits of the gamble.

11. I enclose a statement of this case in tabular form prepared by Mr. Yeh Yuan Chang, 4th. Assistant A.

(Enclosure 2.)

I have the honour to be,

Sir,

Your obedient Servant,

R. F. C. Hedgeland

Commissioner.

APPENDIX 11.

AIGUN NO. 159 TO I.G.

APPENDIX 1.

Translation.

From Dalcentrosoyus, Amur District, Blagovestchensk, to Aigun Commissioner.

Delegation of
Dalcentrosoyus,
Amur District.
Blagovestchensk.
17th September, 1923.
No. 201.
Telephone No. 93.

To,
The Taheiho Customs,
Taheiho.

Herewith enclosed we are sending you letter No. 7445 of 16th August, 1923, received from Centrosoyus (ENGLAND), Ltd., Harbin.

The enclosed documents are in support of our application from the Taheiho Customs for drawback on duties amounting to Mex. $ 23,187.40.

Please send your reply to the Russian Representative at Taheiho.

(signed) Timkin.
Delegate of Centrosoyus, Amur District.

Translation made by:
Wang [signature]
2nd Clerk, C.

APPENDIX 2.

AIGUN NO. 159 TO I.G.

APPENDIX 2.

" Declaration " (Letter No. 7445 of 16th. August, 1923,) from Harbin branch of the " All-Russian" "Central Union of Consumers' Societies."

Всероссiйскiй
ЦЕНТРАЛЬНЫЙ СОЮЗЪ
Потребительныхъ Обществъ
Сибирское Отдѣленiе
Харбинское Представительство
г. Харбинъ,
уг. Бульварной и Стрѣлковой, с.д.
Телефоны:
общiй---------------№ 21-61
кабин. управляющ. № 22-61
каб. пом. управл. № 23-61
торговаго отдѣла № 25-61
Управленiе Дальневосточными
Конторами
В.Ц.С.П.О. въ г. Чита.
№ 7445

Харбинъ 16th August дня 1923 года.

To

The Chinese Maritime Customs

at Helampo.

DECLARATION.

From the attached hereto Costom house receipts No. No. 145, 272, 273, 1091, 1244, 2210, 3645, 3646, 3652, 3653, 3656, 3657, 3665, 3673, 3649, 3647, 3650, 3648, 3655, 3076 and 3651, the original Bills of Lading and also from the information supplied by the Chinese Commercial Union of Harbin, under No. 556 dated April 28th. 1922, you will note that an overcharge was made on the above mentioned receipts for an amount of Twenty three thausand, one hundred and eighty seven dollars and forty cents / M.D. 23,187.40/ which sum kindly refund to us.

Enclosures;-

1. 21 Custom house receipts,
2. Statement of reckoning,
3. 24 Specifications
4. 24 copies of invoices,
5. Copy of information of the Chinese Commercial Union No. 556 dated 28th, April. 1922.
6. Letter of the Russo-Belgian Company dated April 17th 1923, regarding the right of Centrosouis to receive the

AIGUN NO. 159 TO I.G.

APPENDIX 2.

(continued)

the overcharge made.

truly Yours

ALL-RUSSIAN CENTRAL UNION

OF CONSUMERS' SOCIETIES (Signed) V. Nemchinoff.

True Copy:

Wang K'ai-mao

2nd Clerk, C.

APPENDIX 3.

AIGUN NO. 159 TO I.G.

APPENDIX 3.

" Statement of Reckoning "

STATEMENT OF RECKONING

NN of receipts	Received	Overcharge
145	195.04	115.39
272	3057.21	1834.90
273	1386.00	846.00
1091	168.64	15.50
1244	434.58	61.98
2210	237.50	32.09
3645	2348.50	1433.50
3646	770.00	430.00
3652	3638.25	2273.25
3653	492.80	188.80
3656	5274.50	3219.50
3657	1078.00	238.00
3665	1159.60	434.47
3655	2387.00	917.00
3673	1901.90	931.90
3676	154.00	94.00
3649	4620.00	2094.00
3647	2695.00	1295.00
3650	5735.73	3535.73
3688	2444.71	1142.55
3651	1796.35	1083.85

ALL RUSSIAN CENTRAL UNION
OF CONSUMERS' SOCIETIES
(Signed) V. Nemchinoff.

True Copy:
[signature]
2nd Clerk, C.

APPENDIX 4.

AIGUN NO. 159 TO I.G.

APPENDIX 4.

Translation.

哈爾濱商務總會
Chinese
Chamber of Commerce.
Harbin,
28th April, 1922.
No. 556.

INQUIRY
at the request of the Russo-Belgian Co.

Extarct of Letter of 3rd February, 1921, to Commercial Department, Chinese Eastern Railway Company:

In reply to Letter No. 314 of 22nd January, 1922:-

(1) Blue Sheeting Cotton Wadded Trousers-per pair-$ 2.80-weight $2\frac{3}{4}$ Rus. lbs.
(2) Grey Sheeting Cotton Wadded Trousers-per pair-$2.80 -weight $2\frac{3}{4}$ Rus. lbs.
(3) Black Sheeting Cotton Wadded Trousers-per pair-$2.80-weight $2\frac{1}{4}$ Rus. lbs.
(4) Blue Nankeen Trousers -per pair -$ 2.00 - weight $1\frac{1}{2}$ Rus. lbs.
(5) Black Nankeen Cotton Wadded Trousers-per pair-$2.80-weight 2 5/8 Rus. lbs.
(6) Black Nankeen Cotton Wadded Trousers-per pair-$2.60-weight $2\frac{1}{2}$ Rus. lbs.
(7) Black Drill Trousers -per pair -$0.70-weight $0\frac{3}{4}$ Rus. lbs.
(8) Blue Sheeting Shirt -per piece- $0.70- weight $0\frac{3}{4}$ Rus. lbs.
(9) Drill - per piece -$12.00 - weight 12 Rus. lbs.
(10) Black Sheeting Cotton Wadded Coat-per piece-$2.60 - weight $2\frac{3}{4}$ Rus. lbs.
(11) Black Drill Cotton Wadded Coat-per piece-$2.80-weight 3 Rus. lbs.
(12) Black Drill Cotton Wadded Coat-per piece-$2.60-weight $2\frac{3}{4}$ Rus. lbs.
(13) Black Drill Cotton Wadded Trousers-per pair-$2.50-weight $2\frac{1}{2}$ Rus. lbs.
(14) Grey Sheeting Cotton Wadded Coat-per piece-$2.50-weight $2\frac{1}{2}$ Rus. lbs.
(15) Black Drill - per piece -$ 13.00 - weight 12 Rus. lbs.
(16) Black Sheeting -per piece-$12.00 - weight 12 Rus. lbs.
(17) Black Clothing Material-no information can be given.
(18) Blue Drill Cotton Wadded Coat-per piece-$2.60-weight $2\frac{1}{2}$ Rus. lbs.
(19) Black Sheeting Cotton Wadded Coat-per piece-$2.60-weight $2\frac{3}{4}$ Rus. lbs.
(20) Black Drill Cotton Wadded morning gown -per piece-$1.80-weight $1\frac{3}{4}$ Rus. lbs.
(21) Black Drill Cotton Wadded morning gown-per piece-$2.00-weight 2 Rus. lbs.
(22) Black Drill Cotton Wadded Coat-per piece-$2.70-weight $2\frac{1}{2}$ Rus. lbs.
(23) Blue Drill Cotton Wadded Trousers-per pair-$2.50- weight $2\frac{1}{2}$ Rus. lbs.
(24) Grey Drill Cotton Wadded Trousers-per pair-$2.50 -weight $2\frac{1}{2}$ Rus. lbs.
(25) Blue Drill Cotton Wadded morning gown-per piece-$5.00 weight 4 Rus. lbs.
(26) Blue Drill Cotton Wadded morning gown-per piece-$5.30 (large size)

AIGUN NO. 159 TO I.G.

APPENDIX 4.

Translation.
(continued)

(large size).
(27) Black Drill -per piece - $ 15.00 -weight 13 Rus. lbs.
(28) White Sheeting -per piece -$10.00- weight 11 Rus. lbs.

(signed) Signature illegible.
President.

(signed) Signature illegible.
Secretary.

Seal of
Chinese Chamber
of Commerce,
Harbin.

True Translation:
Wang Ki-nan
2nd Clerk, C.

APPENDIX 5.

AIGUN NO. 159 TO I.G.

APPENDIX 5.

Translation.

Translation from the Russian.

To The All Russian Central Union of Consumers Societies
" Centrosouis"
Harbin.

I herewith confirm, that during the years 1920 and 1921, the former Russian-Belgian Trading Company, in whose service I was as Manager of affairs, transported your merchandise in Sahalian, and on export of said merchandise to Blagovestchensk, the Company paid the Customs duties with your monies.

In addition to sundry other goods, the Company paid duties on your goods to the Sahalian Customs under the following Customs quittances in 1920; No.3647 for the sum of Lan 1750.000, No. 3648-1587.500, No. 3650-3724.500, No. 3651-11027.500. No.3649-3000.000, No. 3673-1235.000, No. 3076-100.000, No. 3656-3425.000, No. 3645-1525.000, No. 3652-2363.500, No. 3657-700.000, No. 3653-320.000, No. 3655-1550.000, No. 3665-753.000, No. 3654-500.000, and in the year 1921; No. 69 for the sum of Lan 12.500, No. 272-1985.200, No. 1090-62.920, No. 2210-151.415, No. 109-109.505, No. 273-900.000, No.270-389.180, No. 271-387.585, No. 145-126.650, and No.1244 for the sum of Lan 282.194.

The duty on all the above stated quittances was paid out of your funds and for your account, therefore, all rights to the recovery of any excess amounts charged for duty belongs to you.

(signed) The former Manager of the former Russo-Belgian Trading Company. I.E.Brizin.

I

AIGUN NO. 159 TO I.G.

APPENDIX 5.

Translation.
(Continued)

I, the below signed, certify that the above signature was made in my presence, Ivan Timofeivitch Dmitrieff, Harbin Notary, in my office situated in house No. 8, Yamskaya street, by the personally known to me and living in Harbin, citizen Issai Efimovitch Drizin.

Harbin, 1923, this 17th. day of April. Register No. 2233.

(signed) Notary Iv. Dmitrieff.

Notary Seal.

True Copy:

2nd Clerk, C.

APPENDIX 6.

AIGUN NO. 159 TO I.G.

APPENDIX 6½

Acting Tidesurveyor's Memorandum of 18th October, 1923.

Sir,

With reference to the appended Price List handed into this Office by the Central Commercial Union covering a large consignment of Cotton Wadded Uniforms re-exported to Blagovestchensk in 1920-21 to supply the Red Army, now claimed to have been over-valued by the Taheiho Customs.

I have the honour to report that these goods were examined and passed by Mr. Wahlgren, Chief Examiner, before my arrival here therefore it is almost impossible for me to give a value on goods that I have never seen, especially with Wadded Clothing as there are so many kinds, values varying according to quality of material they are made from, I notice that this list gives prices for ordinary Native Cotton Clothing (not Uniforms) which existed in 1922 and not in 1920 and 1921 when there was a great and urgent demand for warm uniforms to supply the Troops, owing to which, the prices went up considerably not only on clothing but goods in general.

In 1922 the market price for a Cotton Wadded Suit made from ordinary Dyed Shirting or Sheeting was $ 5.80 per suit (value given on price list from the Central Commercial Union $ 5.60 very near our value) but for a Cotton Wadded Uniform made from the same material

was

AIGUN NO. 159 TO I.G.

APPENDIX 6.
(continued)

was $9.00 per suit which equals Hk.Tls. 5.75 less 12% merchants profits would equal Hk.Tls. 5.06 per suit value given by Mr. Wahlgren was Hk.Tls. 5. per suit so I fail to see that these goods were over-valued.

The above mentioned prices are local market prices and not Harbin prices but the prices between Harbin and here could not exceed more than Hk.Tls. 0.50 per suit.

According to the Applications all these goods came overland via Tsitsihar by carts and the Central Commercial Union did not take into consideration the heavy Freight Charges which are three to four times dearer than steamer Freights also the Surtax which was included in the duty assessed there is no doubt that if all these overland freight charges are properly looked into which should have been included in the value of the goods a Debit note should be issued to this firm for additional duty.

Furthermore it seems very stange that a large concern like the Central Commercial Union should have paid duty on their goods throughout the winter of 1920 and not complained and now after over Two years have elapsed they find out that they have been overcharged.

(Signed) G.E.Baukham,
Acting Tidesurveyor.
(Examiner, A.)

Acting Tidesurveyor's Memorandum of 20th.October,1923.

AIGUN NO. 159 TO I.G.

APPENDIX 6.
(Continued)

Acting Tidesurveyor's Memorandum of 20th October, 1923.

Sir,

In continuation of my memo. concerning goods Re-exported to Blagovestchensk by the Central Commercial Union, said to have been over-valued by the Taheiho Customs.

I cannot find any values for the undermentioned commodities in the value book for 1920-21 but the values shown below are for 1922-23 as follows:-

	Hk.Tls.	
Sheep-skin Coats Long	10-12	According to quality
" " " Short	6-10	" " "
Leather Knee Boots	5-10	" " "
Fur Hats for Soldiers or Workmen	1-1.50	" " (Russian Style).
Leather Belts	0.50-1.00	" to quality
Fur Gloves for workmen	0.40-1.00	" " "

For the rest of the items mentioned on the appended list, the exporters values have been taken.

Yours Obediently,
(Signed) G. M. Baukham,
Acting Tidesurveyor.
(Examiner, A.)

True Copies
Wang yue-sil
3rd Clerk C.

APPENDIX 7.

AIGUN NO. 159 TO I.G.

APPENDIX 7.

Aigun Commissioner to Delegate of (Dal)Centrosoyus, Amur District, Blagovestchensk.

CUSTOM HOUSE,

Aigun/Taheiho, 30th October, 1923.

Sir,

I am directed by the Commissioner of Customs to state that your letter of 17th September, 1923, asking for a refund of $23,187.40, which amount you claim to have been over-charged by this Office on various consignments of winter clothing, etc., imported in 1920 and 1921, has been duly received, and to confirm the reply, given verbally several weeks ago, that the Revenue Accounts of this Office for these two years have long ago been closed and that your request cannot be granted.

Enclosures Nos. 1, 3, 4, 5 and 6 of Letter No.7445 dated 16th August, 1923, addressed to this Office by Centrosoyus (England), Ltd., Harbin, are herewith returned

I am,

Sir,

Your obedient Servant,

(Signed) Yeh Yuan Chang,

B/O Commissioner of Customs.

To

The Delegate of Centrosoyus,

Amur District,

Blagovestchensk.

Russian Version.

True Copy:

[signature]

2nd Clerk, C.

AIGUN NO. 159 TO I.G.

APPENDIX 8.

Translation.

From Dalcentrosoyus, Amur District, Blagovestchensk, to Aigun Commissioner.

Delegation of
Dalcentrosoyus,
Amur District.
Blagovestchensk.
27th February, 1924.
No. 177.
Telephone No. 328.

To,
The Commissioner of Customs,
Aigun.

Reply to Aigun Commissioner's letter of 30th October, 1923:

We hereby beg to inform you that we have claimed refund of duties for the following reasons:-

(1) During 1920 and 1921, when our goods were re-exported, the Aigun Commercial Treaty of 1886 between China and Russia was still in force and according to this Treaty, the export from China to Russia of Native goods such as leather ware, Shoes, Belts, etc., if made in foreign style, are to be passed free of duty. Similarly, foreign goods, which are never required to pay duty when sent out of China are to be passed free.

(2) There was appended to the Additional Agreement for the promotion of the trade of the Treaty Port of Aigun, signed in Peking in 1914 by the Inspector General of Customs and the Russian Minister, a Special Duty Free List in which native goods entitled to be passed free were given in detail. To supplement this Agreement,

AIGUN NO. 159 TO I.G.
APPENDIX 8.
Translation.
(Continued)

Agreement, the Harbin Commissioner of Customs and the Russian Consul-General came to an arrangement concerning Customs procedure for refund of duties on above mentioned goods. Our goods were re-exported during the time when this Agreement was still in force, and as the Aigun Customs was then a sub-station of the Harbin Customs, it follows that the Aigun Office must abide by the above Agreement.

(3) The Customs rule fixes the time-limit of Duty Receipts for foreign goods at 3 years. When our first letter of 17th September, 1923 was written the time-limit had not expired, and we are not aware that the public has been notified that this rule is cancelled.

(4) The practice in the Harbin Customs District is as follows:-

If a Duty Receipt bears a remark made at any of the Customs sub-stations of the Harbin District to the effect that the cargo has been re-exported, this is regarded as sufficient proof that the merchant is entitled to refund of duty. Everyone of our Duty Receipts bears a remark to this effect and some of them give full particulars about the goods.

We are not aware that any subsequent rule has been issued which cancels the above practice.

(5) When the Aigun Custom House was opened, the public was notified that foreign goods and native goods on the Duty Free List, when sent overland from Tsitsihar to Blagoveschensk through the Aigun Customs, would be passed free of duty. Our goods on which refund of duty is claimed are entitled to the benefit of the above procedure, and under the authority of these rules, we beg you to refund duty collected on the following Aigun Customs Duty Receipts:-

No.

AIGUN NO. 159 TO I.G.
APPENDIX 8.
Translation.
(Continued)

No.	Amount Mex. $
3652	3,638.25
2210	237.19
1244	434.58
1090	96.90
1091	168.64
145	195.04
3876	154.00
3673	1,901.90
273	1,386.00
3646	770.00
3656	5,274.50
3655	2,387.00
3657	1,078.00
3645	2,348.50
272	3,057.21
3647	2,695.00
3649	4,620.00
3648	2,444.75
3650	5,735.73
3651	17,906.35
3653	492.80
3665	1,159.63
Total: Mex. $	58,181.97

Enclosure: 22 Duty Receipts.

(Signed) Timkin.
Manager of Dalcentrosoyus,
Blagovestchensk.

Translation made by:
Wang Tin-...
2nd Clerk, C.

APPENDIX 9.

~~Aigun Commissioner to Manager of Dalcentrosoyus.~~

AIGUN NO. 159 TO I.G.

APPENDIX 9.

Aigun Commissioner to Manager of Dalcentrosoyus, Blagovestchensk.

CUSTOM HOUSE,

Aigun, 2nd. April, 1924.

Sir,

I have duly received your letter of 27th. February, 1924, *in re* request for refund of duty on cargo re-exported during 1920 and 1921. I note the arguments upon which you base your claim, but am of the opinion that circumstances alter cases and take the opposite view. A merchant has a right, in certain circumstances, to demand a drawback, but a Custom House has always an equal right to demand the opportunity to satisfy itself that the cargo in question is entitled to drawback privilege. Your application for Drawback should have been made at the time when the cargo was re-exported. I am reporting this case to the Inspector General of Customs for instructions.

I enclose a Russian rendering of this letter.

Yours faithfully,

(Signed) R. F. C. Hedgeland,

Commissioner of Customs.

The Manager,

Dalcentrosoyus,

Blagovestchensk.

True Copy:-

Wang I-man

2nd Clerk, C.

Russian Version.

[A—29]

No. 173. COMMRS. INSPECTORATE GENERAL OF CUSTOMS,

Aigun. No. 98,713. PEKING, 7th May 1924.

Entered in Card-Index.

Sir,

I have to acknowledge receipt of your despatch No. 159 :

reporting that you have rejected a claim from the Dalcentrosoyus for refund of duties amounting to $58,181.97;

and, in reply, to say that, although the firm's claim for the Drawback is not tenable, the line adopted by you in refuting the claim is open to criticism.

The outstanding feature of this case is the fact that neither the original Import Application nor the Re-export Application bore any particulars of marks or numbers - the essential factors for the identification of original packing which is a sine qua non for the issue of Drawback. This absence of marks

and

The Commissioner of Customs,

A I G U N.

and numbers is the more important, seeing that the cargo was not declared for re-exportation to Blagovestschensk but for importation into Taheiho where, as reported in your despatch, it was stored for some time outside Customs control, so that no proof exists that the cargo was ultimately re-exported in original packages.

It is on this ground that you should have informed the firm that their claim for Drawback could not be entertained and, although you acted correctly in informing their representative that values accepted in 1920 and 1921 cannot be arbitrarily altered in 1924, this is a side issue as compared with the fundamental principle of the absence of marks and numbers. A further side issue is represented by the applicant's failure to apply for Drawback at the time of re-exportation.

Where, however, you displayed an error of judgment was in informing the firm, both verbally and in writing, that the Revenue Accounts for

the

the years 1920 and 1921 were closed and that their request for Drawback could not be granted. This statement opens the door to the charge that Customs officials are ignorant of their own procedure, in addition to being contrary to fact and misleading. It is contrary to fact because Drawbacks, when properly issuable, are deducted from the Revenue of the current year in which they are issued, so that the closing of a previous year's Revenue Account does not affect the question; and it is misleading because it is liable to be interpreted as meaning that Drawback was otherwise issuable.

Should the firm renew their application for Drawback, I have to instruct you to inform them that the absence of marks and numbers on the Export and Re-export Applications, and the resultant absence of proof that the cargo re-exported was identical with that imported, preclude issue of Drawback.

The

The 22 Duty Receipts enclosed in your despatch are returned herewith.

I am,

Sir,

Your obedient Servant,

F. W. Maze

Inspector General.

呈海关总税务司署159号文　　　　　　　　　　瑷珲关1924年4月7日

尊敬的海关总税务司(北京):

1. 今年年初,全俄消费合作社中央联社(All-Russian Central Union of Consumers' Societies,简称为"俄中央联社")社远东分社(Dalcentrosoyus)[①]来函要求瑷珲关退还此前对其货物所征之税款,共计58181.97银圆。

苏俄中央联社远东分社曾于1920年11月、12月及1921年1至4月间经由陆路通过齐齐哈尔及梁家屯将货物分批运入大黑河,又于1921年1至6月间将货物分批复出口至布拉戈维申斯克(Blagovestchensk)。然其于复出口时,并未申请退税,因此并无证据证明货物复出口时可享退税特权,仅有凭证可证明货物复出口时为免税通行。本署遂驳回退税要求,并告知此事将呈报海关总税务司。

2. 在具体说明该58181.97银圆退税要求(1924年2月27日收到退税要求信函)之前,本署需先对1923年10月俄俄中央联社提出的23187.40银圆退税要求事予以阐明。

俄中央联社曾于1920年11月、12月及1921年1至6月间经由陆路通过齐齐哈尔及梁家屯将冬服、靴子等军需品运入大黑河,并于1921年1月1日至6月30日将货物分批复出口至布拉戈维申斯克,后于1923年来函称,瑷珲关当年估税时,为其货物估值过高,提出退税要求,为此,其哈尔滨分社还发来"声明书"(附录2"1923年8月16日第7445号信函")作为佐证。该"声明书"附有:

(1)21份完税收据;

(2)估算报表;

(3)24份明细表;

(4)24份发票副本;

(5)1922年4月28日哈尔滨商务总会(Chinese Commercial Union)[②]第556号信息抄件;

(6)1923年4月17日俄比公司(Russo-Belgian Company)关于俄中央联社有权索要海关征收之超额关税事的信函(附英文译本);

兹附22份完税收据(附件1),以供查验。须说明,中央联社[③]1923年9月17日来

---

① 该名称乃据其俄文所译,dalcentrosoyus为其俄文音译之英文,其中dal有远东之意,centrosoyus为中央联社。

② 此呈附录4中载有其中文哈尔滨商务总会,信息号与时间皆与此处相符,唯附录中英文为Chinese Chamber of Commerce, Harbin。

③ 此处英文为the Union,应为All-Russian Central Union of Consumers' Societies的简写,故简译为中央联社。

函（要求退税 23187.40 银圆）中附有 21 份完税收据，1924 年 2 月 27 日来函（要求退税 58181.97 银圆）中却附有 22 份完税收据。

另附：

（1）上述（2）估算报表抄件（英文）（附录 3）；

（2）上述（5）1922 年 4 月 28 日哈尔滨商务总会第 556 号信息抄件（俄文），附瑷珲关所制英文译本（附录 4）；

（3）上述（6）1923 年 4 月 17 日俄比公司关于俄中央联社有权索要海关征收之超额关税事的信函抄件（俄文），附俄中央联社所制英文译本（附录 5）；

此外，上述（3）24 份明细表及（4）24 份发票副本均已返还。

3. 本关已对此事进行仔细调查，署理头等总巡于其报告（附录 6）中指出：

（1）普通棉衣套装与棉衣制服价格有别；

（2）1922 年与 1920 年及 1921 年物价有别；

（3）哈尔滨与大黑河市场物价有别，尤其是在需耗巨资将货物经陆路运至大黑河的冬季。

此外还需注意：

（1）中央联社将发票价值视为征税价值，忽视了仍有各种额外费用的事实；

（2）若根据发票价值计算所征税款，则所报 21 份超额征税收据中，仅有 11 份数据相符；

（3）完税收据所附票据中有不完整，甚至错误者；

（4）第 3651 号完税收据所附票据不完整，交至瑷珲关的中文报单与存档的英文报单所载信息不一致；

（5）有 3 份收据将附加税与关税混为一谈；

（6）所有货物几乎均由报关行公济栈代为申报，其认同申报价值低于海关估值，但对于海关估值过高这一说辞并未认同；

（7）报单上既无标记亦无号数，且无凭证可证明原包装上有标记及号数，若将中央联社申报为原装复出口之货物送至验货厂重新检验，本关亦不会认同其为此前放行之货物；

（8）估算报表所列超额征收税款总计 22217.41 银圆，而中央联社索要之数额为 23187.40 银圆。

4. 为谨慎起见，本署在至中央联社的回函（附录 7）中并未据理力争，而是尽量少言，但已向其前来索要退款的代表说明，海关验货之原则便是消除质疑，若要重新审议海关估值，则须重新验货，但 1920 年 12 月及 1921 年 1 月之估值既已被接受，瑷珲关自不会于 1923 年 10 月再同意将之更改，而且 1920 年及 1921 年账目已结，不可能满足其更改之请求。

对于该退税要求，本署一直以来的态度都是一笑置之。兹认为，本关验货员于 1920 年末做出之判断不应受货主 1923 年 10 月提出之质疑所影响，而且海关并无义务请商人申请退税，若其不申请，海关则将其视为永久放弃。因此，应让那些为谋取私利而妄图篡改海关规定之人承认“既成事实”，不得扰乱规则。

5. 本署曾希望此事可到此为止，然未遂人愿，退税申请金额已由最初的 23187.40 银圆涨至 58181.97 银圆（附录 8），简直难以想象，而且退税原因已不再是因货物估值过高而导致的超额征税。

俄中央联社在 1924 年 2 月 27 日来函中要求瑷珲关将对其相关货物所征税款悉数退还，并对此抱有很大希望，然其申请提交日期已然太迟，无法证明是否可享退税。但中央联社认为，凡商人享有退税特权者，无论何时，均可于方便之时申请退税，而海关之利益则无关紧要。其态度似乎是在表明：“海关既有按照条约规定退税之义务，我们便来要求海关履行此义务。”此即为该问题之核心。

本署已回函（附录 9）说明反对退税之理由，指出货物复出口三年后再申请退税有违海关原则，即凡申请退税者，海关均有权要求其提供充分证据证明其申请合理；凡未申请退税者，无论是何动机，海关均假定其货物不享有退税特权；更何况其货物已重新打包，就相当于此前从未送交海关查验。海关须时刻防范那些肆无忌惮专门骗取税收之徒，且于当前状况而言，退税风险过高。

6. 俄中央联社于 1924 年 2 月 27 日来函中强调了以下几点内容：

（1）根据 1886 年《瑷珲通商条约》规定，凡洋货及洋式土货自中国运往俄国者，均享有免税特权。

（2）海关总税务司与俄国公使于 1914 年在北京所签附加协议中载有免税名单，哈尔滨关亦予以认可，且货物复出口至俄国时，此协议仍有效，瑷珲关当时作为哈尔滨关之分关理应予以认可；

（3）退税时限为三年，瑷珲关收到退税申请时并未超过此时限；

（4）凡完税收据上载有海关关员备注之货物已复出口之说明者，哈尔滨关均将之视为货物享有退税特权之证明；

（5）瑷珲关初设时，已告知公众凡洋货及洋式土货经陆路通过齐齐哈尔出口至俄国者，均免税通行。

对此，兹认为：

（1）中央联社意欲参照1881年《圣彼得堡条约》，但应注意，货物复出口时并未交纳出口税。而且瑷珲关既已无法复验货物，要求退税一方又无法证明有权享此退款，58181.97银圆之退税要求自然无法应允。此外，并无证据可证明货物为原装复出口，且其报单上又无标记及编号，货物当时运往布拉戈维申斯克时是否能证明为原装复出口都令人质疑。不过，其洋货复出口时免税通行十分合理，因验货员已确信货物为洋产；土货免纳出口税同样合理，因皆为洋式且属免税名单之列。然此事之关键在于当时运往布拉戈维申斯克之货物是否即为于运抵大黑河时完纳进口税者。而今此事已无从证实，退税之事实属无稽之谈；

（2）货物既已无法辨别，又何来退税之说。而且进口报单大多不会注明土货为洋式；

（3）按照规定，凡洋货符合必要条件者，如于抵达口岸后三年内复出口，均可享受退税，但此规定不可解释为，商人若忘记于复出口时申请退税，还可于货物离开口岸两三年后在其方便之时申请退税。且因洋货享免税复出口，故若商人未于复出口时申请退税，本关有时则不会仔细查验货物即予以放行；但对于申请退税之洋货，必会严格查验，其中标记和号数为重点审核之项。此乃海关惯例，海关不应被迫做出妥协，放弃原则；

（4）瑷珲关于完税收据上记录之备注，仅说明货物持有完税收据，或其中部分货物已复出口，并提醒不得再就此货物做任何申请，但并不能证明复出口之货物在包装、标记及号数等方面皆与原进口之货物一致，不能证明货物可享退税特权；

（5）中央联社的土货之所以可自大黑河免税运往布拉戈维申斯克，乃因其为中俄两国间的直接运输；而其土货经陆路通过齐齐哈尔及梁家屯运抵大黑河时需交纳进口税，是因1）此非中俄两国间的直接运输。2）货物运抵本口后并未申报将运往布拉戈维申斯克；至于其洋货，征收进口税乃因货物未申报将复出口至俄国，运往俄国布拉戈维申斯克时免税放行，乃因海关确信货物为洋产。其洋货及土货均于大黑河存放过一段时日，且不在海关管辖范围以内。

7. 俄中央联社或许认为本关拒绝其退税申请乃背离海关惯例，然其货物是否可享受退税特权，实难验证。如以下两例。

（1）1921年12月，前铃子手西多处（E.S.Sidortchook）先生申请对其于1920年7月进口并于1920年9月复出口至布拉戈维申斯克的洋货退税。但已遭拒绝，因1）其未于复出口时申请退税；且2）货物缺少标记及号数，无法证明复出口之货物即为原进口之货物；

（2）报关行公济栈此前于1924年2月11日经陆路通过齐齐哈尔和梁家屯进口4件橡胶轮胎及4件汽车用钢制弹簧，运抵后即刻申报8件货物将复出口至布拉戈维申斯克，本关遂征收35银圆押款以抵应征之进口税，并于8件货物上加盖铅印。然当其于1924年2月19日请准复出口，并申请退税时，本关却发现8件货物均已开封，铅印业已去除，轮胎及弹簧均已被安装在车上，故以货物无法辨别且进口税已入账为由，拒绝退税。

兹认为，该两案均证明，本关确应于退税前慎重行事。

8. 若海关完税收据可作退税凭证，中央联社之退税申请便可允准，但完税收据仅可证明某些货物复出口时获免税通行，却无法证明货物当时是否为原装复出口。

若就此同意退税，日后会有何影响，恐怕亦非今日所能预料。申请人于1920年及1921年或许有，也或许没有退税特权，但因货物复出口至今时日过长，亦只能凭借推测来判定。而海关目前面临之问题已远远不止是，是否应于1924年无条件退还该笔大额钱款，而是，是否应接受未经证实的公众陈词代替确凿证据。

海关此次若不拒绝中央联社的退税要求，必会为日后提供无法容忍的判例，瑷珲关之处境亦会十分尴尬，对进口后又复出口至布拉戈维申斯克之货物所征之税款只怕均会以存票之形式退还回去。

瑷珲关1918年、1919年及1920年税收较高，分别为161646、128893及海关两188526海关两，乃因战争所致的虚假繁荣现象，当时由于西伯利亚大铁路停止运输货物（军需品除外），大黑河顺势成为货物集散中心，所有货物运至布拉戈维申斯克后，均可销售出去。这三年复出口至俄国的货物总值增长迅速，远非战前所能及。以下为统计数据：

1915年至1922年复出口至俄国货物总值

年份	海关两（两）	年份	海关两（两）
1915	358153	1919	2212525
1916	251874	1920	3582686

1917	1497190	1921	1484682
1918	2587930	1922	1126507

同时,战争期间货物进口总值亦增长显著,从 1915 年 3044839 海关两增至 1918 年 7446438 海关两,1919 年 7151682 海关两及 1920 年 7042905 海关两。

从这些数据中可以看出,这三年货物进口量虽大幅增长,但并非因本埠所需,货物大多运至主要依靠大黑河市场供货的布拉戈维申斯克地区。

据悉,大黑河一些商人因手中持有进口后又复出口至俄国之货物的完税收据,正打算向瑷珲关提出退税要求。对于此等行为,海关唯有坚持原则,要求退税申请必须于复出口时提出,方可制止;若应允中央联社之要求,必会有更多商人提出退税申请,海关将陷入无尽的混乱,甚至闹剧之中。

9. 俄中央联社乃政府贸易公司,对于退税之事或将坚持到底,甚至有向北京方面提出抗议之可能。而且,布拉戈维申斯克政府资金严重紧张,很有可能会于背后施加影响强制退税。

然兹认为,于此事而言,瑷珲关行为合情合理,相反在此情况下提出退税要求既不正当,亦不合理。中央联社远东分社经理应该知道,海关依照规定办事,退税申请既已推迟三年,海关有权以最基本、最重要的税收利益为优先考虑,正如其以中央联社利益为重一样。若其为明理之人,自应理解这一点,应当意识到其退税要求在缺乏合理证据的情况下必会被驳回。

10. 此外,前钤子手西多处先生现居于大黑河,此次退税事很有可能乃此人在背后谋划煽动,甚至可能有人承诺事成之后分其利益,此绝非臆想。

11. 兹附四等帮办前班叶元章所制报表(附件 2)。

您忠诚的仆人

贺智兰(R. F. C. Hedgeland)

瑷珲关税务司

瑷珲关致海关总税务司署第159呈附录1

布拉戈维申斯克阿穆尔地区俄中央联社远东分社致瑷珲关税务司信函译本

兹附俄中央联社哈尔滨分社[①]1923年8月16日第7445号信函，以作本公司向大黑河海关申请退税总计23187.40银圆之证明文件。

回函请寄至驻大黑河俄国代表处。

（签字）迪金（Timkin）

阿穆尔地区中央联社代表

翻译人：王德懋　二等同文供事后班

① 此处英文为Centrosoyus（ENGLAND），Ltd.，Harbin，在孙修福先生的《近代中国华洋机构译名大全》中查有Centrosojus（England），Ld.译作（英商）俄国协助会洋行，并注明其总公司位于伦敦，分公司位于上海1919、汉口。然附录2信函仍为Harbin branch of All-Russian Central Union of Consumers' Societies，故于此将Centrosoyus统一译作中央联社，与前后文保持一致。

瑷珲关致海关总税务司署第159呈附录2

俄中央联社哈尔滨分社“声明书”
(1923年8月16日第7445号信函)

1923年8月16日,哈尔滨

尊敬的大黑河中国海关:

兹附海关收据第145、272、273、1091、1244、2210、3645、3646、3652、3653、3656、3657、3665、3673、3649、3647、3650、3648、3655、3076及3651号,提单原件及1922年4月28日哈尔滨商务总会(Chinese Commercial Union)第556号信息抄件,从中可知,贵署此前超额征税,望退还总计23187.40银圆之税款。

附件:

1. 21份完税收据;
2. 估算报表;
3. 24份明细表;
4. 24份发票副本;
5. 1922年4月28日哈尔滨商务总会第556号信息抄件;
6. 1923年4月17日俄比公司关于中央联社有权索要海关征收之超额关税事的信函。

您真挚的

俄中央联社

(签字)尼姆吉诺夫(V. Nemchinoff)

该抄件内容真实有效,特此证明:

录事:王德懋　二等同文供事后班

瑷珲关致海关总税务司署第159号呈附录3

估算报表

收据编号	已收金额	超征金额
145	195.04	115.39
272	3057.21	1834.90
273	1386.00	846.00
1091	168.64	15.50
1244	434.58	61.98
2210	237.50	32.09
3645	2348.50	1433.50
3646	770.00	430.00
3652	3638.25	2273.25
3653	492.80	188.80
3656	5274.50	3219.50
3657	1078.00	238.00
3665	1159.60	434.47
3655	2387.00	917.00
3673	1901.90	931.90
3676	154.00	94.00
3649	4620.00	2094.00
3647	2695.00	1295.00
3650	5735.73	3535.73
3688	2444.71	1142.55
3651	1796.35	1083.85

俄中央联社

(签字)尼姆吉诺夫(V. Nemchinoff)

此译本内容真实有效,特此证明:

确认人签字: 王德懋　二等同文供事后班

瑷珲关致海关总税务司署第159号呈附录4

1922年4月28日哈尔滨商务总会①第556号信息抄件译本

哈尔滨商务总会

1922年4月28日

第556号信息

应俄比公司(Russo-Belgian Co.)要求提供:

自1921年2月3日致中东铁路公司商务部(Commercial Department, Chinese Eastern Railway Company)之信函中摘录。

回复1922年1月22日第314号信函:

(1)蓝色床单布棉裤,每条2.80银圆,重2.75俄磅

(2)灰色床单布棉裤,每条2.80银圆,重2.75俄磅

(3)黑色床单布棉裤,每条2.80银圆,重2.75俄磅

(4)蓝色南京棉布裤,每条2.00银圆,重1.5俄磅

(5)黑色南京棉布棉裤,每条2.80银圆,重2.375俄磅

(6)黑色南京棉布棉裤,每条2.60银圆,重2.5俄磅

(7)黑色斜纹棉布裤,每条0.70银圆,重0.75俄磅

(8)蓝色床单布衬衣,每件0.70银圆,重0.75俄磅

(9)斜纹棉布,每块12.00银圆,重12俄磅

(10)黑色床单布棉衣,每件2.60银圆,重2.75俄磅

(11)黑色斜纹棉布棉衣,每件2.80银圆,重3俄磅

(12)黑色斜纹棉布棉衣,每件2.60银圆,重2.75俄磅

(13)黑色斜纹棉布棉裤,每条2.50银圆,重2.5俄磅

(14)灰色床单布棉衣,每件2.50银圆,重2.5俄磅

(15)黑色斜纹棉布,每块13.00银圆,重12俄磅

---

① 呈文中商务总会对应英文为Chinese Commercial Union,此附录中英文为Chinese Chamber of Commerce, Harbin。

（16）黑色床单布，每块 12.00 银圆，重 12 俄磅

（17）黑色衣料，无信息

（18）蓝色斜纹棉布棉衣，每件 2.60 银圆，重 2.5 俄磅

（19）黑色床单布棉衣，每件 2.60 银圆，重 2.75 俄磅

（20）黑色斜纹棉布加棉晨衣，每件 1.80 银圆，重 1.75 俄磅

（21）黑色斜纹棉布加棉晨衣，每件 2.00 银圆，重 2 俄磅

（22）黑色斜纹棉布棉衣，每件 2.70 银圆，重 2.5 俄磅

（23）蓝色斜纹棉布棉裤，每条 2.50 银圆，重 2.5 俄磅

（24）灰色斜纹棉布棉裤，每条 2.50 银圆，重 2.5 俄磅

（25）蓝色斜纹棉布加棉晨衣，每件 5.00 银圆，重 4 俄磅

（26）蓝色斜纹棉布加棉晨衣，每件 5.30 银圆（大号）

（27）黑色斜纹棉布，每块 15.00 银圆，重 13 俄磅

（28）白色床单布，每块 10.00 银圆，重 11 俄磅

（签字）

主席

（签字）

秘书

哈尔滨商务总会印章

此译本内容真实有效，特此证明：

确认人签字：王德懋　二等同文供事后班

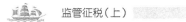

瑷珲关致海关总税务司署第 159 号呈附录 5

1923 年 4 月 17 日俄比公司关于俄中央联社有权索要海关征收之超额关税事的信函译本

（译自俄语版）

致俄中央联社哈尔滨分社：

兹确认，前俄比贸易公司曾于 1920 年及 1921 年期间将贵公司货物运至大黑河，后出口至布拉戈维申斯克，并以贵公司之钱款交纳关税。在此期间，本人于前俄比贸易公司事务部任经理。

俄比贸易公司为贵公司货物向大黑河海关交税的收据列下：

1920 年完税收据第 3647 号（金额 1750.000）、第 3648 号（金额 1587.500）、第 3650 号（金额 3724.500）、第 3651 号（金额 11027.500）、第 3649 号（金额 3000.000）、第 3673 号（金额 1235.000）、第 3076 号（金额 100.000）、第 3656 号（金额 3425.000）、第 3645 号（金额 1525.000）、第 3652 号（金额 2363.500）、第 3657 号（金额 700.000）、第 3653 号（金额 320.000）、第 3655 号（金额 1550.000）、第 3665 号（金额 753.000）及第 3654 号（金额 500.000）；

1921 年完税收据第 69 号（金额 12.500）、第 272 号（金额 1985.200）、第 1090 号（金额 62.920）、第 2210 号（金额 151.415）、第 109 号（金额 109.505）、第 273 号（金额 900.000）、第 270 号（金额 389.180）、第 271 号（金额 387.585）、第 145 号（金额 126.650）及第 1244 号（金额 282.194）。

上述收据所载关税皆以贵公司资金结付，业已记入贵公司账户，因此任何索要超额关税之权利皆归贵公司所有。

（签字）前俄比贸易公司经理

德里津（I. E. Drizin）

本人，即署名者，德米特列夫（Ivan Timofeivitch Dmitrieff），为哈尔滨公证人，特此证明，上述签字为现居于哈尔滨的公民德里津亲笔所书，签字地点为本人位于亚姆斯卡亚街 8 号的办公室内。

于 1923 年 4 月 17 日哈尔滨，登记号：2233。

（签字）德米特列夫

（盖章）公证人

此译本内容真实有效，特此证明：

确认人签字：王德懋　二等同文供事后班

瑷珲关致海关总税务司署第159号呈附录6

1923年10月18日瑷珲关署理头等总巡报告

尊敬的瑷珲关税务司：

根据中央联社此前提交之关于1920年及1921年复出口至布拉戈维申斯克供苏维埃红军所用之棉衣制服的价格表（称大黑河海关估值过高），兹报告，该批货物乃由头等验货华格伦（O. W. Wahlgren）先生负责查验并放行。当时本人尚未至瑷珲关任职，故无法为从未见过之货物估价，尤其所涉布料种类繁多，材料质量亦不尽相同。

但本人发现，此表所载乃为1922年普通棉衣套装（非棉衣制服）之价格，1920年及1921年由于军队急需保暖制服，棉衣制服的价格大幅上涨，就连其他货物的价格亦因此而节节攀升。

1922年，普通棉衣套装（由普通染色细纺或染色平布制成）市价为5.80银圆每套（中央联社价格表所列为5.60银圆每套），然同等面料制成之棉衣制服市价为9.00银圆（5.75海关两）每套，扣除12%商人利润，价格为5.06海关两每套，华格伦先生所给估价为5海关两每套，由此可见海关估值并未过高。

上述价格均为本埠市价，而非哈尔滨市价，不过，两地差价应不会超过0.50海关两每套。

根据报单可知，货物皆经陆路由货车通过齐齐哈尔运至此地，中央联社未考虑到此举较之轮船运费高出三至四倍，更未考虑到海关估税中已含附加税。而且，海关为货物估值时本应将所有陆路运费计算在内，若如此，恐怕海关还须向该公司签发仍欠账单，收取额外税费。

此外，着实令人费解的是，像俄中央联社此等大公司，若果真于1920年冬季完纳所有货物之关税，为何当时未曾控诉，反倒在时隔两年后发现海关征税过高。

（签字）博韩（G. E. Baukham）

瑷珲关署理头等总巡

（二等验货前班）

1923年10月20日瑷珲关署理头等总巡报告

尊敬的瑷珲关税务司:

续本人关于俄中央联社投诉大黑河海关对其复出口货物估值过高事之报告。

1920年及1921年估值簿上并未有下列商品之价格,谨将1922年及1923年估值簿所载价格列下:

	海关两(两)	
长款羊皮大衣	10–12	根据质量
短款羊皮大衣	6–10	根据质量
及膝皮靴	5–10	根据质量
士兵或工人用毛皮帽子	1–1.50	根据质量
皮带	0.50–1.00	根据质量(俄式)
工人用毛皮手套	0.40–1.00	根据质量

随附清单所列其他货物价值均按出口商所给列明。

您忠诚的仆人

(签字)博韩(G. E. Baukham)

瑷珲关署理头等总巡

(二等验货前班)

此译本内容真实有效,特此证明:

录事: 王友燮 三等同文供事后班

瑷珲关致海关总税务司署第159号呈附录7

瑷珲关税务司致布拉戈维申斯克阿穆尔地区俄中央联社远东分社代表函

瑷珲关/大黑河1923年10月30日

尊敬的布拉戈维申斯克阿穆尔地区俄中央联社代表：

奉瑷珲关税务司命令，谨告知，贵公司1923年9月17日来函已收悉。此函中声称，瑷珲关对贵公司于1920年及1921年进口之冬季衣物征税过高，要求退还23187.40银圆税款。

现进一步确定几周前之回复，瑷珲关1920年及1921年税收账户已结，无法批准退税请求。

随函退还俄中央联社哈尔滨分社发送至瑷珲关之1923年8月16日第7445号信函附件1、3、4、5及6。

您忠诚的仆人

（签字）叶元章

奉瑷珲关税务司命令代签

此译本内容真实有效，特此证明：

录事：王德懋　二等同文供事后班

瑷珲关致海关总税务司署第159号呈附录8

布拉戈维申斯克阿穆尔地区俄中央联社远东分社致瑷珲关税务司函译本

[布拉戈维申斯克 Blagovestchensk]，1924年2月27日

尊敬的瑷珲关税务司：

为回复瑷珲关税务司1923年10月30日信函：

兹告知，本公司要求退税理由如下：

（1）本公司货物于1920年及1921年复出口期间，中俄签订之1886年《[瑷珲通商条约》仍有效。据此条约，由中国出口至俄国之土货，如皮革制品、鞋、皮带等，若为洋式，均免税通过。同样，洋货运出中国时亦免税通行。

（2）为促进瑷珲通商口岸贸易，海关总税务司与俄国公使于1914年在北京签订附加协议，协议所附免税名单中已详细列明可免税通行之土货。为补充此协议，哈尔滨关税务司与俄国总领事亦就此类货物的退税办法达成协定。本公司货物复出口时，此协议仍有效，且瑷珲关当时仍为哈尔滨关分关，故亦应予以遵守。

（3）海关规定的洋货完税收据时限为3年。而本公司首封退税申请信函写于1923年9月17日，仍在期限内；且据本公司所知，目前尚未有公告称此规定已取消。

（4）哈尔滨关区之惯例如下：

凡完税收据上载有哈尔滨关区任一分关备注之货物已复出口之说明者，均可作为货物享有退税特权之证明。

本公司完税收据皆载有此类备注，更有附注货物详情者。且据本公司所知，目前尚未有取消上述惯例之规定。

（5）瑷珲关初设时，已告知公众，凡洋货及免税名单所载土货经陆路通过齐齐哈尔出口至布拉戈维申斯克者，均免税通行。本公司要求退税之货物均享有退税特权，请贵署按照规定根据以下瑷珲关完税收据退税：

完税收据编号	金额
	墨西哥银圆
3652	3638.25

完税收据编号	金额
	墨西哥银圆
2210	237.19
1244	434.58
1090	96.90
1091	168.64
145	195.04
3876	154.00
3673	1901.90
273	1386.00
3646	770.00
3656	5274.50
3655	2387.00
3657	1078.00
3645	2348.50
272	3057.21
3647	2695.00
3649	4620.00
3648	2444.75
3650	5735.73
3651	17906.35
3653	492.80
3665	1159.63
总计：	58181.97

附件：22 份完税收据

（签字）迪金（Timkin）

布拉戈维申斯克

俄中央联社远东分社经理

翻译人：王德懋　二等同文供事后班

瑷珲关致海关总税务司署第159号呈附录9

瑷珲关税务司致布拉戈维申斯克阿穆尔地区俄中央联社远东分社经理函

瑷珲关1924年4月2日

尊敬的布拉戈维申斯克俄中央联社远东分社经理：

贵公司1924年2月27日来函已收悉，函中请求对1920年及1921年复出之口货物退税。

关于贵公司退税申请之理由，本署无法认同。兹以为，凡事须依情况而定，在某些情况下，商人固然有权利要求退税，然海关亦有权要求申请人证明货物的确可享退税特权。而且贵公司退税申请本应于货物复出口时提出。本署已将此案呈报海关总税务司，以待指令。

兹附此函俄文译本。

您忠诚的仆人

贺智兰（R. F. C. Hedgeland）

瑷珲关税务司

此译本内容真实有效，特此证明：

录事：王德懋　二等同文供事后班

致瑷珲关第 173/98713 号令 海关总税务司署（北京）1924 年 5 月 7 日

尊敬的瑷珲关税务司：

第 159 号呈收悉：

“已拒绝俄中央联社远东分社金额为 58181.97 银圆的退税要求。”

现批复如下：该公司退税的要求虽不合理，但贵署的驳斥方法很容易引人非议。

此案例的关键在于，货物原进口报单及复出口报单上均没有任何特殊标记或序号，难以鉴别原包装，而这恰恰是退税必不可少的条件。缺少标记和序号是更为重要的原因。由于货物报关并非复出口到布拉格维申斯克，而是进口至大黑河。正如贵署呈文所示，在此期间，货物存储有一段时间并不受海关控制，因此没有证据可以表明该货物最终是否还以原包装复出口。

基于此，贵署理应通知该公司的退税要求无法满足。贵署曾告知该公司代表 1920 和 1921 年认可的课税价格不能在 1924 年随意更改，这一理由虽然正确，但相比缺少标记及序号的基本原则问题，这只是一个次要问题。另一个次要问题是报关人未能在货物复出口时申请退税。

在这一点上，贵署无论是口头还是书面，都向该公司传达了一个错误的消息，即由于 1920 年与 1921 年税收账户关闭，其退税请求不能予以批准。这一说法不仅为指控海关官员无视办事规程大开方便之门，而且有悖于事实，容易引起误解。有悖于事实，是因为退税予以发放时均从当年税收账下扣款，且在当年完成发放，所以上年度税收账户关闭与此问题没有干系；容易引起误解，是因为这样解释表明退税还可以有其他发放方式。

如果俄中央联社远东分社更新其退税报单，贵署应通知其出口及复出口报单上缺少标记和序号，从而导致缺乏证据表明复出口货物与进口货物一致，有碍退税发放。

随函返回贵署呈中的 22 份完税收据。

您忠诚的仆人

安格联（F. A. Aglen）

海关总税务司

6. 为请示可否为运往大黑河的糖签发特别免重征执照事

SERVICE No. 19

No. 1 Aigun

Reg. No. 678

CUSTOM HOUSE,

NEWCHWANG, 12th. June, 1922.

Sir,

I have been approached by the local agents of Messrs. Butterfield and Swire with reference to the issue of Special Exemption Certificates covering sugar destined for Taheiho.

Copy of an extract from Messrs. Butterfield and Swire's letter is appended for your information, and I beg to request that you will inform me whether the statements contained therein as to the status of Taheiho are correct, and whether Special Exemption Certificates for sugar destined for Taheiho are issuable.

I am,

Sir,

Your obedient Servant,

R. L. Warren

Acting Commissioner.

The Commissioner of Customs,

AIGUN.

Appendix

Appendix.

Newchwang , 8th. June , 1922 .

R. L. Warren , Esquire ,

Commissioner ,

Chinese Maritime Customs ,

NEWCHWANG .

Dear Sir ,

Sugar forwarded to Taheiho. It has been customary for the Customs here to refuse Exemption Certificates for sugar forwarded to Taheiho on the ground that Aigun and not Taheiho is the Treaty Port .

In this connection our Harbin office write us as follows :-

"We would mention that on taking up the matter with the Commissioner of Customs at Taheiho , we are informed that it has been laid down by the Inspector General that Taheiho and Aigun are to be treated as one place so far as the issue of E.Cs. is concerned . A Custom House is in existence at Taheiho and in any case the Japanese and Foreign Firms importing via Dairen are granted E.Cs. to Taheiho . Importers via Newchwang are entitled to equal treatment and we shall be obliged if you will kindly take up the question with the Customs at yours and arrange for a drawback of the Transit Pass Duty already paid." etc., etc.

We are , Sir ,

Yours faithfully ,

per pro BUTTERFIELD & SWIRE
(John Swire & Sons, Ltd.)

(Signed) R. K. Rodger .

True copy :

[signature]

4th. Assistant, B.

致瑷珲关第 1/678 号函　　　　牛庄关 1922 年 6 月 12 日

尊敬的瑷珲关税务司:

太古洋行(Messrs. Butterfield and Swire)本地代理近日向本署询问有关运往大黑河的糖签发特别免重征执照之事。

兹附太古洋行信函摘要抄件,以供参考。望告知函中关于大黑河之陈述是否正确?是否可为运往大黑河的糖签发特别免重征执照?

您忠诚的仆人

(签字)霍李家(R. L. Warren)

牛庄关署理税务司

附录

牛庄关 1922 年 6 月 8 日

尊敬的牛庄关税务司霍李家（R. L. Warren）先生：

为糖运往大黑河事：牛庄关一直以通商口岸是瑷珲而非大黑河为由，拒绝为运往大黑河的糖签发特别免重征执照。

关于此事，太古洋行哈尔滨办事处来函称：

“哈尔滨办事处已向大黑河海关税务司咨询此事，得知海关总税务司署已有规定，凡涉及免重征执照签发之事，瑷珲与大黑河均应视为一地。而且大黑河已设有海关。根据现行惯例，凡日本及其他洋行之货物经大连关进口运往大黑河者，均获签发免重征执照；凡进口货物经牛庄关运往大黑河者，亦享有此待遇。遂请向当地海关说明此事，申请退还子口税。”

您忠诚的仆人

（签字）罗杰（R. K. Rodger）

谨代表太古洋行签署

该抄件内容真实有效，特此证明：

录事：四等帮办后班

7. 为运送到国外港口的洋货从国外复进口时征税办法事

72.

I. G.

Aigun Taheiho 30th September, 1922.

Sir,

I have the honour to report that on 2nd August the Taheiho firm Hsi Shêng Tai (西盛泰) imported from Blagovestchensk, per Barge "Kirbi" - belonging to the "Rupvod" (Russian Government Water Transports) - 4500 tins kerosene oil, 352 empty tins and 154 bags millet, which cargo was found on examination to be damaged. The importers declared that this cargo was part of a shipment exported from Harbin in 1921, loaded on Barge No. 153, towed by S. S. "Irkutsk" - also belonging to the "Rupvod" - Barge No. 153 having been sent to Habarovsk instead of Taheiho.

From records it was verified that S.S. "Irkutsk", which cleared in October 1921 from Harbin,

towing

To

The Inspector General of Customs,

PEKING.

towing barge No. 133 with 6000 c/s kerosene and 426 bags millet, arrived in Taheiho without the barge, which was reported as having been sent to Habarovsk for fear the steamer be delayed on the road and caught by the ice in some desert place on the river; regular documents issued by the Harbin Customs, covering the goods loaded on barge No. 133 were handed to this Customs through the Steamer "Irkutsk".

There was no proof, however, that the Kerosene Oil and Millet imported on 2nd August 1922 by Barge "Kirbi" be the same that were originally shipped - duly covered by documents - at Harbin per barge No. 133; I therefore ruled that Import Duty should be levied on Kerosene - Millet being free by tariff. But the merchant asked to be allowed to produce further proof of his contention and I allowed him - provisionally and pending reference of the case to you - to deposit a guarantee made out by two reliable firms, for payment of duty if so decided by you. After a few days the merchant handed in a declaration by the

Commercial

Commercial Navigation Department of the Amur Government, which certified to having taken to Habarovsk Barge No. 133, and having trasferred the cargo - or rather what remained after requisition by the Russian Military Authorities - to Barge "Kirbi", which brought the goods to Taheiho via Blagovestchensk (translation enclosed).

There is no provision in the Customs Regulations for re-importation from abroad ; strictly speaking import duty is leviable on goods imported from abroad, irrespective of their origin. However I believe that the peculiar nature of this frontier, and the circumstances of the case may justify a special treatment. The Certificate of the "Rupvod" is a strong proof, and is corroborated by other facts and documents; and I would be in favour of remitting duty to the already hard-hit merchant. - I have therefore the honour to solicit your instructions in a matter which is not unlikely to occur again in this District.

I have the honour to be, Sir,

Your obedient Servant,

G. Boch.

Acting Commissioner.

Enclosure in Aigu despatch No. 72 to I. G.

Direction of Amur Government
Navigation Commercial Department

22nd August, 1922
No. 205
Blagovestchensk.

CERTIFICATE.

The present Certificate is issued to the Chinese firm Hsi Shèng Tai to the effect that goods as per Kupvod Bills of lading No. 47 (426 bags millet = 2700 poods) and No. 48 (6000 tins kerosene oil = 6000 poods) were despatched on 5th October 1921 by Barge No. 133 in tow of Str. Irkutsk from ~~Habarovsk~~ Harbin to Taheiho. In view of the late season, and for fear of having to winter in a desert tract of the river, the said goods were sent to Habarovsk for the winter. Her part of the goods were requisitioned by instructions of the Delegate to the evacuation, before the evacuation of troops in December 1921, as follows :-

1058 tins = 1058 poods, kerosene

1750 poods millet

Afterwards, in the present year, after the opening of navigation, the remaining goods were loaded on Barge Kirbi for Blagovestchensk, the quantity being 4534 tins = 4250 poods kerosene oil, 400 empty tins and 154 bags = 950 poods and 12 lbs millet.

The said goods were delivered to the firm Hsi Sheng Tai at Taheiho, and according to the papers made out by both parties the quantities handed over were: 4500 tins kerosene, weight 4015 poods 5 lbs., 352 empty tins, weight 38 poods 28 lbs., and 154 bags millet, weight 942 poods 12 lbs.

The shortage in the weight of goods received at the time of handing them over is explained by incorrect tare, as well as to leaky tins and to the poor quality

and

and weakness of part of the bags.

The Manager of Steamers

(signed) Tokareff

(seal) The Director of the Commercial Department

(signed) Bogoluvskoi

I hereby certify to the signatures of Manager of Steamers Tokareff and Director of the Commercial Section Bogoluvskoi.

For the Director General

(signed) Engeneer Lagutin

30/VIII/1922.

==================

True Translation,

Acting Commissioner.

...—27e]

...83 Commrs.

Inspectorate General of Customs,

Aigun No. 91,598

PEKING, 18th October, 1922.

SIR,

I am directed by the Inspector General to acknowledge receipt of your Despatch No. 72 :

reporting the circumstances in which certain foreign goods shipped from Harbin to Aigun had been sent to a foreign port (Habarovsk) from which a portion of them had subsequently been re-imported at Aigun, and suggesting that, though import duty is strictly speaking leviable on these goods as arriving from abroad, the special circumstances of the case might justify a remission of this duty;

and, in reply, to say that your report does not give full information with regard to that portion of the original cargo, as shipped from Harbin, which failed to arrive at Aigun, and that without this information the Inspector General is unable to consider fully the merits of the case.

The

Commissioner of Customs,

A I G U N.

The amount of kerosene oil originally shipped from Harbin for Aigun would seem to have been 6,000 tins, and these are reported to have arrived at Habarovsk : 1,058 tins are said to have been requisitioned at Habarovsk, leaving a balance of 4,942 tins : only 4,534 tins of oil are certified to have been loaded at Habarovsk on the barge "Kirbi" for Blagovestchensk : of the 4,534 tins said to have been loaded at Habarovsk, only 4,500 tins of oil arrived at Aigun. The number of empty tins which arrived at Aigun, and from which the oil may have leaked, as it is said, does not completely explain the discrepancies noted; but in any case your despatch does not deal with the question of the empty tins as it should have done. You are requested therefore to supply as full information as possible on the above points.

Your attention is also called to what appears to be a typewriting error in line 6

of

of of the enclosure in your despatch under reply: Habarovsk would seem to have been written for Harbin.

I am,

Sir,

Your obedient Servant,

Chief Secretary.

80.

I. G.

Aigun/Taheiho 20th November, 1922.

Sir,

I have the honour to acknowledge the receipt of your despatch No. 85/91,598 :

calling for further information re Foreign Goods shipped at Harbin to Taheiho, and sent by shipping Company to a foreign Port, and subsequently re-imported ;

and, in reply, to say that I have obtained a certified copy of a farther statement issued by the Amur Water Transports (Rupvod) showing in details how the original cargo is accounted for; a translation of the document is enclosed.

I must point out, and regret, that another typewriting error, besides the one brought to my notice in your despatch under reply, has crept in

my

The Inspector General of Customs,

PEKING.

my despatch No. 72, and that line 5 of the first page should read 352 empty tins, not 382.

The story therefore goes as follows: 1) 6000 tins were shipped at Harbin; 2) a shortage of 15 was found out on arrival at Habarovsk, leaving a balance of 5,985; 3) at Habarovsk, 1051 tins (not 1058 as stated in the previous document of the Rupvod) were requisitioned, thus reducing the balance to 4,934, which, as already reported, were shipped from Habarovsk (4,534 full, 400 empty); 4) again, on the way, 82 were lost, and 4,852 tins (4,500 more or less full, 352 empty) were handed over to the consignee, as verified by our examination. - The 82 tins lost on the way from Habarovsk to Taheiho are reported as "apparent shortage from ullage and leakage", but that does not explain the disappearance of the empty tins; and, in fact, the Rupvod, while refusing to accept a claim for all damages, alleging force majeure, are ready to indemnify for the loss of these 82 empty tins and for the 15 tins which were found missing on arrival at Habarovsk.

That two documents issued by the Water Transports do not entirely tally, is not to be

wondered

wondered at, this Administration not being quite efficient; a small mistake can also be detected in the total weight of the Kerosene requisitioned, which is reported (and should be) 1051 poods and 11 lbs., while the sum of the single requisitions comes to 1051 poods, and 26 lbs. - But these minor mistakes do not, in my opinion, nullify the value of the documents, as showing that the same cargo actually, and by force of circumstances beyond the control of the merchant, were sent to Habarovsk in the first instance, and re-shipped this year for theor original destinatio Taheiho.

As to the empty tins, their treatment should, in my opinion, be the same as the one you decide to grant to the Kerosene: although the tins have not paid duty separately at Harbin, they are covered by the fact that duty on Kerosene in tins is considerably higher than on Kerosene in Bulk.

I have the honour to be,

Sir,

Your obedient Servant,

G. Bochi

Acting Commissioner.

[A—27 e]

No. 98 Commrs.

Aigun No. 92,327

Inspectorate General of Customs,

PEKING, 11th December, 19 22.

SIR,

I am directed by the Inspector General to acknowledge receipt of your Despatch Nos. 72 and 80 :

Foreign goods shipped from Harbin to Aigun and sent by Shipping Company to a foreign port: duty treatment of on re-importation from abroad: circumstances reported and instructions solicited;

and, in reply, to state as follows :

Although the facts may be as stated, the Certificates produced do not seem to be altogether reliable and the organisation which issued them is reported by you to be inefficient. But even so, there are 97 tins of oil and the contents of 352 other tins not satisfactorily accounted for. Moreover, the S.S. " Irkutsk " which left Harbin in October 1921 towing the barge on which the oil was loaded, duly completed her voyage, and

reported

The Commissioner of Customs,

 A I G U N.

reported at Taheiho, but without the barge, the latter having been deliberately sent to Habarovsk for fear, it is said, that she might dangerously delay the steamer's progress. In the conditions of the river which then existed the barge should not have left Harbin in tow of the steamer. However, the risk was deliberately taken and the resultant penalties can hardly be expected to be avoided. The Inspector General considers that if refund of the duty properly leviable on the oil - which, as you report, could not be identified as that originally shipped at Harbin - were granted, an undesirable precedent, affording opportunity for malpractices, would be created. Duty is leviable on the oil and the tins as imported at Taheiho and should be collected. Refund of the duty taken on deposit cannot therefore be allowed.

I am,

Sir,

Your obedient Servant,

Cecil A. V. Bowra

Chief Secretary.

呈海关总税务司署 72 号文　　　　瑷珲关 / 大黑河 1922 年 9 月 30 日

尊敬的海关总税务司（北京）：

兹报告，大黑河西盛泰商行于 8 月 2 日自布拉戈维申斯克（Blagovestchensk）由俄阿穆尔国家水运局的“基尔比”（kirbi）号驳船运入 4500 桶煤油、352 个空桶及 154 袋谷子，之后于查验时发现货物有受损之状况。西盛泰商行称此批货物乃 1921 年其委托俄阿穆尔国家水运局另一艘轮船“立古次”（Irkutsk）号所拖拽之第 133 号驳船自哈尔滨关运出之部分货物，但当时第 133 号驳船并未至大黑河而是直接被送往哈巴罗夫斯克（Habarovsk）。

根据记录已核实，“立古次”号轮船于 1921 年 10 月在哈尔滨关办理结关时的确拖拽装有 6000 桶煤油、426 袋谷子的第 133 号驳船，但轮船抵达大黑河时，驳船并未一同而至，据悉是因担心轮船行程会有延误，受到浮冰围困，故将驳船直接送至哈巴罗夫斯。由哈尔滨关签发之第 133 号驳船载货凭照当时已由“立古次”号轮船于抵达大黑河后上交瑷珲关。

只是并无证据可证明“基尔比”号驳船于 1922 年 8 月 2 日所载煤油及谷子确系第 133 号驳船此前自哈尔滨关所运，本署因此下令向煤油征收进口税，谷子可按税则规定免税。随后，西盛泰商行请求批准其出示其他证据，本署遂决定在将此案呈交至海关总税务司署期间，允许其先寻得两家可靠商行为其担保，再由总税务司决定是否征税。数日后，西盛泰商行提交了一份由阿穆尔国家水运局商务部（Commercial Navigation Department of the Amur Government）为其开具之证明书，证明第 133 号驳船确曾被运送至哈巴罗夫斯克，后将货物，确切地讲，是俄国军方征用后剩余之货物，转由“基尔比”号驳船经布拉戈维申斯克运送至大黑河（随呈附上证明书及其译本）。

然海关章程中并无有关自国外复进口之条款，严格而论，凡货物自国外进口者，无论产地，均应征收进口税。不过，鉴于边境性质特殊，此事或可特案特办，而且俄阿穆尔国家水运局所提供之证明证据确凿，又与海关凭证所载相符，本署支持免于向已受严重打击的西盛泰商行征税。鉴于瑷珲关区日后或将再次发生同类事件，特此请求贵署予以指示。

您忠诚的仆人

包安济（G. Boezi）

瑷珲关署理税务司

瑷珲关致海关总税务司署第72号呈附件

阿穆尔国家水运局商务部指令　　　　　　　1922年8月22日,布拉戈维申斯克

证明

此证明签发予中国商行西盛泰,谨证明,俄阿穆尔国家水运局第47号提单(426袋谷子=2700普特)及第48号提单(6000桶煤油=6000普特)所列货物于1921年10月5日由"立古次"号轮船所拖拽之第133号驳船自哈尔滨运往大黑河,但因已到航运季末,担心轮船会受浮冰围困,故将第133号驳船连同货物送至哈巴罗夫斯克过冬。该批货物后被当地部队征用,至1921年12月部队撤离时,征用货物明细如下:

煤油,1058桶=1058普特

谷子,1750普特

今年航运开通后,剩余货物由"基尔比"号驳船运往布拉戈维申斯克,包括4534桶(4250普特)煤油,400个空桶,154袋(950普特12磅)谷子。

上述货物随后运至大黑河西盛泰商行,如双方凭据所示,交接货物数量包括4500桶煤油(重4015普特5磅)、352个空桶(重38普特28磅)及154袋谷子(重942普特12磅)。

交接时货物数量有所短缺乃因皮重计算有误,油桶漏油,部分包装袋质量不够结实。

轮船公司经理

(签字)托卡乐福(Tokareff)

(盖章)商务部部长

(签字)博古卢夫斯科伊(Bogoluvskoi)

兹证明,轮船公司经理托卡乐福及商务部部长博古卢夫斯科伊签字有效。

代表阿穆尔国家水运局督办

(签字)(工程师)拉古丁(Lagutin)

1922年8月30日

致瑷珲关第83/91598号令　　　　海关总税务司署1922年10月18日,北京

尊敬的瑷珲关税务司:

第72号呈收悉:

"瑷珲关遇到如下情形:有些原定目的地为瑷珲关的洋货自哈尔滨关用船运送至国外口岸(哈巴罗夫斯克),之后其中部分货物又复进口到瑷珲关。瑷珲关认为,虽然严格来讲,对这些由国外进口的货物,可以征税,但此次情况特殊,捐税免除理由尚属正当。"

奉总税务司命令,现批复如下:兹告知,贵署汇报中没有全面给出这批始发于哈尔滨关但未抵达瑷珲关的原始货物信息,若没有这些信息,海关总税务司无法对该案例作出权衡。

似乎最初从哈尔滨关运往瑷珲关的煤油总计6000桶,据报告称都已抵达哈巴罗夫斯克;其中在哈巴罗夫斯克军队征用1058桶,剩余4942桶;经证实在哈巴罗夫斯克装到"基尔比"号驳船上运到布拉格维申斯克的只有4534桶油;而声称在哈巴罗夫斯克装到船上的4534桶油,只有4500桶煤油抵达瑷珲关。抵达瑷珲关的空罐的数量有问题,可能因为半路有泄漏,但不能解释罐子总数不一致;贵署呈文中并未解释清楚空罐问题,这是应尽的职责。因此,贵署须就以上几点尽可能给出全面的信息。

还请贵署注意,贵署呈文附件第六行有一处打字错误:哈巴罗夫斯克海关已向哈尔滨关发函。

您忠诚的仆人

包罗(C. A. Bowra)

总务科税务司

呈海关总税务司署 80 号文　　　　　　瑷珲关 / 大黑河 1922 年 11 月 20 日

尊敬的海关总税务司（北京）：

根据海关总税务司署第 83/91598 号令：

"请详细汇报洋货原应自哈尔滨关运至瑷珲关（大黑河）却被船运公司运至外国口岸后又复进口一事。"

兹报告，本署已收到俄阿穆尔水运局关于此批货物的信息证明抄件，内容详尽；随呈附上该证明译本。

另须于此更正，瑷珲关第 72 号呈第一段第五行所载空桶数量应为 352，而非 382；对此打印错误，本署深感抱歉。

该事件具体情况如下：1）轮船于哈尔滨装运 6000 桶煤油；2）抵达哈巴罗夫斯克（Habarovsk）时遗失 15 桶，仅余 5985 桶；3）在哈巴罗夫斯克期间被征用了 1051 桶（并非阿穆尔国家水运局于此前证明中所述之 1058 桶），剩余 4934 桶自哈巴罗夫斯克运出（其中 4534 桶装有煤油，400 桶为空置）；4）运输途中遗失 82 桶，最终交与收货人 4852 桶（其中 4500 桶装有煤油，352 桶为空置），与海关所验之数相符。

自哈巴罗夫斯克至大黑河途中遗失的 82 桶煤油，报明之原因为"耗损及泄漏"，但这并不能解释空桶为何会遗失。实际上，俄阿穆尔国家水运局虽以不可抗力为由拒绝为所有损失做出赔偿，但对于遗失的 82 个空桶及在抵达哈巴罗夫斯克时丢失的 15 桶，已表示愿意予以赔偿。

对于俄阿穆尔国家水运局所签发的两份证明文件略有差异一事，亦不必感到讶异，因该局办事一向效率不高。证明中所列征用煤油总重亦存在误差，总计列明为（且应该为）1031 普特 11 磅，但将单项数据累计相加得出的结果却是 1031 普特 26 磅。尽管如此，兹认为，该证明文件所含价值亦不应被抹杀，毕竟其已证明货物未经商人允许便被送往哈巴罗夫斯克，又于今年重新运至原目的地大黑河。

至于空桶，兹认为，可照海关总税务司批准之煤油处理办法办理，煤油桶此前虽未于哈尔滨关单独交税，但鉴于桶装煤油比散装煤油的税率高出甚多，因此煤油桶之税款实际已包含在所纳关税之中。

您忠诚的仆人

包安济（G. Boezi）

瑷珲关署理税务司

致瑷珲关第98/92327号令　　　　海关总税务司署（北京）1922年12月11日

尊敬的瑷珲关税务司：

第72号及第80号呈收悉：

“航运公司将自哈尔滨关运往瑷珲关的洋货运送到国外港口；从国外复进口上述货物的征税办法；情况报告，并请求下达相关指示。”

奉总税务司命令，现批复如下：

真实情况也许如此，但开具的证明并非完全可靠，根据贵署报告，签署机构也并不称职。此外，还有97桶油以及其他352桶内容物的去向均未妥善记录。“伊尔库茨克”号轮船在1921年10月离开哈尔滨关时拖着装载有油罐的驳船，本应在大黑河完成其旅程并在瑷珲关报关。但在报关时并未发现驳船，据说是因为担心轮船行程严重延误，故意将驳船送到了哈巴罗夫斯克。根据当时河流的情况，轮船不应拖驳船离开哈尔滨。然而，有人故意冒这样的风险，而且也知道难逃罚款。总税务司认为，据贵署的报告称，无法确认煤油是否与最初在哈尔滨装船时的情况相同，若同意退税，可能会开一个不良先河，给渎职行为创造机会。应按照大黑河进口货物对该煤油和油罐进行征税。保税货物税款不予退还。

您忠诚的仆人

包罗（C. A. Bowra）

总务科税务司

8. 为呈交经满洲往来西伯利亚的货物提供过境便利之意见事

74.

I. G.

Aigun/Tahelho 4th October, 1922.

Sir,

With reference to your despatch No. 2927/90,947 to Harbin, and to Harbin despatch in reply No. 2703 (copies of which have been received through the Harbin Office :

concerning a request, by the All-Russian Central Union of Consumers' Societies, for transit facilities for goods passing through Manchuria to and from Siberia ;

I have the honour to offer the following comments on the through transit of goods by Parcel Post and "in the usual manner" by the "Sahalian (Taheiho) - Dairen - Shanghai" route.

1. Postal Parcels. a) The C. P. O. has an arrangement with the Blagovestchensk Post Office for the exchange of letters and newspapers; no arrangement, existing or under discussion, for exchange of

Postal

The Inspector General of Customs,

PEKING.

Postal Parcels;

b) if such postal arrangement is arrived at, existing regulations would justify duty-free treatment of Postal Parcels from a place abroad for another place abroad, in transit through China, under the guarantee of the C. P. O.;

c) It has sometimes happened that furs, covered by Import Duty Receipt issued by our Winter Road Office, have been shipped abroad (London and New-York) by Parcel Post. The furs, however, had been, on importation, taken delivery of by the merchant, away from Customs control, had been freely manipulated and were re-shipped in entirely different packing (the original one consisting generally of a flour bag, without any marks). Anyhow, the goods proved unidentifiable on re-exportation, and no Drawback was issued. - Should however the merchant make arrangements for storing the furs on importation in a suitable godown under Customs supervision, and for repacking them under our control, import duty should, in my opinion, be refunded on re-exportation abroad by Parcel Post.

II. Ordinary Cargo. a) In winter there

is

is no Customs link between this Port and Harbin, except under the form of a Manchurian Special Exemption Certificate, which does not admit of Drawback (your despatches Nos. 928/43,308 and 1293/54,613 to Harbin);

b) In summer, furs are not exported from Blagovestchensk; only supplies from (or through) China for the Centrosoyus are therefore in question. These are fully covered by documents between Harbin and Taheiho, and whatever duty is collected at Harbin on Foreign goods can be refunded on re-exportation from Taheiho to Blagovestchensk, provided the merchants will take the trouble to strictly comply with Customs Regulations, and have their packages marked and numbered. The knot of the question is therefore elsewhere, i.e. in the Customs control of goods between Harbin and Dairen.

Copy of this despatch is sent to Harbin.

I have the honour to be,

Sir,

Your obedient Servant,

G. Boch

Acting Commissioner.

[C.—32 a]

MEMORANDUM.

Commissioner's Office,
CUSTOM HOUSE,
Harbin, 12th October 1922.

To
The Commissioner of Customs,
Aigun.

AIGUN DESPATCH NO. 74 to I.G., copy of which was supplied to this office. The following comments are necessary:

1. Postal Parcels. c) Last paragraph relating to repacking of furs under Customs control and issue of drawback for import duty paid at Winter Road Office on re-exportation abroad: Drawbacks may only be granted under certain conditions and one of these conditions is that the goods remain intact in their original packages with their original identifiable marks and non-recurring numbers unchanged. Foreign cargo which has been repacked loses all re-export privileges, i.e. right to E.C. or drawback. What might justifiably be done in the case of goods from Blago. sent to foreign countries in transit through Chinese Post-office is either exemption from import duty and release under Post-office guarantee, or payment of import duty and refund by drawback on proof of re-exportation abroad being given the Customs (as is now done at Manchouli for furs arriving from Chita already packed and addressed, and posted at the Chinese Post-office Manchouli for tansmission abroad through China and Shanghai).

[signature]
Commissioner.

呈海关总税务司署 74 号文　　　　瑷珲关 / 大黑河 1922 年 10 月 4 日

尊敬的海关总税务司（北京）：

根据海关总税务司署致哈尔滨关第 2927/90947 号令及哈尔滨关所回复之第 2703 号呈（哈尔滨关已将此两份抄件发送至瑷珲关）：

“俄中央联社请求为经满洲往来西伯利亚之货物提供过境便利。”

兹对以邮递包裹及经“库页岛（大黑河）– 大连 – 上海”路线以普通方式寄送之货物，提出以下意见：

1. 邮政包裹

（1）关于信件及报纸传递一项中国邮政局与布拉格维申斯克邮政局早有协定；而邮政包裹之传递尚无已定或正处协商之协定。

（2）若邮政协定得以达成，当境外邮政包裹欲从中国中转复运往境外时，在中国邮政局的担保之下，依照现行规章制度，便可享免税之待遇。

（3）时有持瑷珲关冬令过江检查处所签发的海关进口税收据之皮货，经邮政包裹运往国外（伦敦及纽约）之事。然皮货一经输入，商人便即刻提货，海关再无从管控。商人可随意处理后彻底再包装（原包装多为面粉袋，无任何标记）后复运出。无论何情，货物复出口时已无从辨认，故无退税之事。然若商人愿于海关监督下将输入之皮货妥善存放至仓库，并于瑷珲关监管下再次包装，兹以为，如此经邮政包裹复出口国外之货物可退还其进口税。

2. 普通货物

（1）冬季瑷珲口岸与哈尔滨关之间并无进出口凭证方面的联络，除非持满洲特别免重征执照，而此执照并无退税之许可（参阅海关总税务司署致哈尔滨关第 928/43308 及 1293/54615 号令）；

（2）鉴于夏季布拉格维申斯克并不出口毛皮，故仅自（或经）中国供给俄中央联社之皮货可供讨论。此等货物所持之海关凭证在哈尔滨关至大黑河之间均有效，且若商人能够严格遵守海关章程，携其包裹至海关加印标记编号，则无论哈尔滨关对洋货征收何种税，此等货物自大黑河复出口布拉格维申斯克时均可退税。如此一来，哈尔滨关至大连关之间的往来货物便都在海关的管控中了。

此呈抄件已发送至哈尔滨关。

您忠诚的仆人

包安济（G. Boezi）

瑷珲关署理税务司

通函

由：	致：
哈尔滨关税务司办公室	瑷珲关税务司
1922 年 10 月 12 日	

1922 年 10 月 4 日瑷珲关致海关总税务司署第 74 号呈收悉：

“1. 邮政包裹 c）皮货可于海关监管下再次包装；于海关冬令过江检查处完纳进口税之货物复出口时可予以退税。”

兹认为，仅在货物满足特定条件的情况之下，方可予以退税。条件之一为货物须仍置于原包装内，完整无缺，且原标记可识别、临时编号保持不变。且再包装之洋货不再享有复出口特权（免重征权或退税权）。此外，若货物自布拉格维申斯克输出经中国邮政局中转运至境外，或可免除进口税，并于邮政局担保之下放行货物，或可缴纳进口税，复出口境外时向海关出示复出口凭证后进行退税（此亦为满洲里现行之办法——自赤塔运至满洲里的皮货由中国邮政局满洲里分局打包、填写地址、邮寄，再经中国上海转运至国外）。

贯韦（R. C. L. d’Anjou）

哈尔滨关税务司

9. 为协商经满洲里往来西伯利亚的转口货物可否退税事

COMMRS.

No.91,782

INSPECTORATE GENERAL OF CUSTOMS,

PEKING, 28th October, 1922.

Sir,

With reference to I.G. despatch No.2927/90,947 to Harbin and Harbin despatch No.2703/I.G. in reply, copies of which were sent to you by the Harbin Commissioner :

concerning a request made by The All Russian Central Union of Consumers' Societies for transport facilities for goods passing through Manchuria to and from Siberia, and more particularly with regard to the request for through transit of goods of Russian origin conveyed by parcel post via Sahalian (Taheiho) and Lahasusu to Shanghai for export abroad;

and to your despatch No. 74 :

reporting that the Chinese Post Office at Taheiho has no arrangement for the exchange of postal parcels with the Blagovestchensk Post Office, but that if such an arrangement were arrived at existing regulations would justify duty-free treatment of postal parcels in transit through China;

I

Commissioner of Customs,

AIGUN.

I am directed by the Inspector General to append copy of his despatch No.2779/87,573 to Harbin :

> describing an arrangement by which, in the case of parcels which, having arrived from Russia by rail at the Manchouli Station and paid import duty there, are handed over in their original packages to the Chinese Post Office at Manchouli for conveyance to Shanghai and export from that place to foreign countries, the Chinese Post Office undertakes to assume charge of the parcels at Manchouli and to guarantee that they will be, and to show proof that they have been, re-exported to a foreign country; and the Harbin Commissioner is authorised to issue Drawbacks for the import duty paid at Manchouli on production of such proof of re-export;

and to authorise you to enter into negotiations with the Chinese Post Office at your port with the object of instituting a similar arrangement for parcels arriving from Blagovestchensk for conveyance through the Chinese Post Office to Shanghai and export abroad from that place, the parcels to pay duty at Taheiho and Drawback to be

issued

issued on the necessary proof of re-export to a foreign country having been supplied by the Post Office.

The parcels must of course remain in their original packages and they should be handed over to the Chinese Post Office immediately after passing through the Customs under a procedure similar to that in force at Manchouli with regard to which you should consult the Harbin Commissioner, copy of whose despatch No.2581 describing his original proposals in this matter is appended for your information.

I am,

Sir,

Your obedient Servant,

Cecil A. V. Bowra,

Chief Secretary.

Appendix.

The Inspector General to the Harbin Commissioner.

No.2779 Commrs. Inspectorate General of Customs,
Harbin No.87,573. Peking, 16th January,1922.

Sir,

With reference to your despatch No.2553 : reporting that you have been consistently refusing all requests for issue of drawbacks for foreign goods imported into Manchouli and re-exported abroad by Parcel Post;

and I.G. despatch No.2758/87,288 :

approving your action as reported;

I append, for your information and guidance, copy of Shui-wu Ch'u despatch No.39 received in this connection, as well as the English draft of my reply thereto, from which you will see I state that as I understand the Chinese Post Office is willing to take charge of the parcels at Manchouli and to guarantee that they will be, and show proof that they have been, re-exported to a foreign country, "there will be no danger of creating an awkward precedent if these parcels are treated as under through Bill of Lading, and the Harbin Commissioner is instructed to issue drawbacks on them as soon as the necessary arrangements with the Chinese Post Office have been made by him concerning proof of re-export".

re-export".

You are requested to act accordingly.

I am,

Sir,

Your obedient Servant,

(Signed) F.A.Aglen,

Inspector General.

English draft of I.G's reply to Shui-wu Ch'u despatch No. 39.

The Inspector General finds that ordinary goods imported by rail from Siberia into Manchouli are only accorded a drawback when re-exported to a foreign country, <u>via</u> Dairen say, if they are sent from Manchouli to Dairen under through Bill of Lading.

The parcels of furs now under discussion have, so the Inspector General is informed, not been treated in this way, they were sent, he believes, as ordinary goods by train through Manchouli under Bill of Lading to Harbin and there delivered to the Chinese Post Office. The Inspector General therefore refused Drawbacks.

But the Inspector General understands that the Chinese Post Office is willing to take charge of the parcels at Manchouli and to guarantee that they will be, and show proof that they have been re-exported to a foreign country.

Under these conditions he thinks that there will be no danger of creating an awkward precedent if these parcels are treated as under through Bill of Lading and the Harbin Commissioner is instructed to issue drawbacks on them, as soon as the necessary arrangements with the Chinese Post Office have been made by him concerning proof of re-export.

The Harbin Commissioner to the Inspector General.

No.2581.

I. G.

Custom House,

Harbin, 14th January, 1922.

Sir,

In my despatch No. 2553 I had the honour to bring to your notice that, as there was no provision for the issue of drawbacks for foreign goods re-exported through the Chinese Post Office, I had consequently refused all requests from merchants for drawbacks for parcels containing furs, made up at Chita, forwarded by rail to Manchouli, and without further repacking sent through the Chinese Post Office at Manchouli to America. In I.G. despatch No. 2758/87,288, in reply, my action was approved.

Mr. Ritchie, the Postal Commissioner, for North Manchuria, to whom I communicated the above, called on me a few days ago to ask me to submit the question to you in the following light, as explained in his despatch No. 81, copy of which will be found appended hereto. The Postal Commissioner says that our refusal to issue drawbacks for foreign goods re-exported abroad in their original packages through the Post Office, while the drawback privilege is granted when these same packages are sent as freight, is driving a profitable source of revenue to the Railway to the detriment of the Chinese Post Office, a Chinese Government institution. To satisfy the Customs

that

that the Postal Parcels sent from Manchouli really leave China for America, the Postal Commissioner proposes to forward these parcels in closed bags to Shanghai and promises to provide the Customs with proofs of re-export in the shape of certificates from the Customs Assistant on duty at the Shanghai Post Office. The Postal Commissioner also remarks that as the Customs issues drawbacks on such goods sent as freight it derives no advantage, while the Post Office is losing a handsome revenue.

Mr. Ritchie's views are logical and are well worth considering in the interest of the Chinese Government, and the manner in which he proposes to furnish the Customs with proofs of re-exportation appears quite satisfactory. There is no objection on the part of this office to drawback privilege being granted if the Inspector General is willing to reconsider his decision.

I have the honour to be,

Sir,

Your obedient Servant,

(Signed) R.C.L. d'Anjou,

Commissioner.

Appendix.

Appendix to Harbin despatch No.2581/I.G.

No.81.
General.

Post Office,
Harbin, 6th January, 1922.

Sir,

1. I beg to acknowledge receipt of your despatch No. 1347 of 31st December :

concerning the non-issue of drawbacks for furs imported into Manchouli from Chita, and re-exported to the U.S.A. by parcel post;

and, in reply, to request you to be good enough to bring the following considerations to the notice of the Inspector General.

2. Goods - principally furs- imported into Manchouli from Chita, and re-exported without repacking as freight on through bills of lading to Dairen, for shipment to the United States, are allowed drawbacks on your authority, after receipt of the " Certificate of Re-export" (Customs form C-57) from the Commissioner of Customs at Dairen, certifying that the goods have been " shipped on board " for the United States.

3. You will, I feel sure, agree that furs posted at Manchouli in their original wrappers - i.e. without repacking - sent in closed parcel mails from Manchouli to Shanghai Chinese Post Office, and certified by the Customs Assistant stationed in that office, and in charge of Parcel Duty Collection, as having been " shipped on board " for the United States, are entitled to the same Customs privileges - i.e. issue of drawbacks - as furs paying transport

charges

charges to a company whose revenue does not accrue to the Chinese Government. As you are aware, if these fur parcels were posted at Chita, and transmitted in closed mails through Manchouli to the U.S.A. the question of Chinese Customs treatment would not arise.

4. The refusal to give the same privileges to postal parcels as to goods by freight drives this profitable carriage to the railway, the Chinese Government losing the large revenue from postage; the Customs, thus having to return to the practice of issuing drawbacks for duty collected on goods sent on through bills of lading, secures no advantage. Two of the leading Manchouli fur dealers are at the moment holding up despatch of a large shipment, pending decision on this question of drawbacks for goods by parcel post; if it is decided that articles carried by the Government Post Office are to be discriminated against by another department of the Government, the furs concerned will be forwarded as freight.

5. The American Consul General has also addressed me by despatch in this matter of drawbacks for furs by parcel post, and reply to his communication awaits the result of this despatch.

6. I beg to request your support in this matter of grave concern to the revenues of the Postal Administration.

I am, Sir,
Your obedient Servant,
(Signed) W.W. Ritchie,
Postal Commissioner for North Manchuria.

copies :

A. Sarkes

Assistant Secretary.

致瑷珲关第 87/91782 号令　　　　　　海关总税务司署（北京）1922 年 10 月 28 日

尊敬的瑷珲关税务司：

根据海关总税务司署致哈尔滨关第 2927/90947 号令，哈尔滨关致海关总税务司署第 2703 号呈，副本已由哈尔滨关税务司发至贵署：

“关于俄中央联社对经满洲往来西伯利亚的货物运输工具请求，特别是关于俄国土货经萨哈连（即库页岛）与拉哈苏苏用邮递包裹寄送至上海，再在上海出口到国外的转口货物的运输请求。”

并且根据第 74 号呈：

“大黑河中国邮政局与俄布拉格维申斯克邮政局之间没有邮递包裹邮寄协议，但若有此类协议达成，则根据现有章程，经中国境内转运的邮递包裹可以给予免税放行。”

奉总税务司命令，兹附海关总税务司致哈尔滨关第 2928/90948 号令副本：

“记载了一份协议，根据该协议，凡包裹由俄罗斯用铁路运送至满洲里分关，在满洲里分关完纳进口税后，原装转交至满洲里中国邮政局，由中国邮政局转运至上海，再从上海出口至其他国家，中国邮政局许诺在满洲里接收包裹并且保证包裹确实复出口至其他国家并开具复出口凭单；哈尔滨关税务司收到授权，在看到上述复出口凭单，即可退还在满洲里缴纳的进口税。”

兹授权贵署，与贵港口中国邮政局进行协商，制定类似协议。凡包裹自布拉格维申斯克运至贵口岸，经贵口岸中国邮政局运往上海，再在上海出口至国外，它们在大黑河缴纳包裹进口税，收到中国邮政局提供的复出口至国外的凭单后即可退还税银。

包裹必须保持原有包装，按照类似满洲里分关的现行办法办理完海关报关手续后立即转交至中国邮政局。关于满洲里分关的现行办法，贵署可咨询哈尔滨关税务司，兹附叙述了该事原始提议的哈尔滨关税务司第 2581 号呈，以供参考。

您忠诚的仆人

包罗（C. A. Bowra）

总务科税务司

附件

致哈尔滨关第2779/87573号令　　　　海关总税务司署1922年1月16日,北京

尊敬的哈尔滨关税务司:

根据第2553号呈:

“哈尔滨关一贯坚持驳回对进口到满洲里,又通过邮寄包裹方式复出口至国外的洋货进行退税的一切请求。”

及海关总税务司署第2758/87288号令:

“批准汇报中采取的行动。”

为了便于贵署顺利执行,兹附税务处第39号令副本及海关总税务司署复函的草稿,以供参考。据此所示,海关总税务司了解中国邮政局希望在满洲里收寄包裹的意愿,并且中国邮政局能够保证包裹确实复出口至其他国家并开具复出口凭单,“如果这些包裹能够像联运提单方式处理,那么可以规避出现尴尬局面的风险。哈尔滨关税务司已收到指示,在与中国邮政局订立有关复出口凭单的协议后,即可给予退税”。

敬请遵照此令执行。

您忠诚的仆人

(签字)安格联(F. A. Aglen)

海关总税务司署函复税务处第39号令草稿

海关总税务司发现，自西伯利亚通过铁路方式运入满洲里的普通货物，只有经其他口岸（比如大连关）按照联运提单方式运送、复出口至其他国家时，方可进行退税。

据海关总税务司所知，本次所商谈的皮草包裹的转运方式并非如此，而是像普通货物一样先用火车经满洲里按货运提单方式运输至哈尔滨，然后在哈尔滨转由中国邮政局寄送。因此，海关总税务司驳回退税请求。

但海关总税务司了解中国邮政局希望在满洲里收寄包裹的意愿，并且中国邮政局能够保证包裹确实复出口至其他国家并开具复出口凭单。

鉴于此种情况，他认为如果这些包裹能够像联运提单方式处理，那么可以规避出现尴尬局面的风险。哈尔滨关税务司已收到指示，在与中国邮政局订立有关复出口凭单的协议后，即可给予退税。

呈海关总税务司署 2581 号文　　　　　　　　哈尔滨关 1922 年 1 月 14 日

尊敬的海关总税务司：

在第 2553 号呈中已上报，关于经由中国邮政局邮寄复出口的洋货，因目前尚无退税规定，故本署已驳回商人对赤塔制造的皮草通过铁路运输至满洲里，再在满洲里经邮政局邮寄转运出口至美国的包裹退税的一切要求。海关总税务司署第 2758/87288 号令的批复已批准本署行动。

本署已向北满邮务管理局李齐（Ritchie）先生沟通此事。几天前邮务长致电，要求本署将其第 81 号函阐述的观点呈报贵署，已附该函副本，以供参考。主要观点如下：邮务长认为，海关拒绝对经由邮政局邮寄的复出口至国外的原装洋货实施退税，但同样的包裹，以货运方式运送则予以退税优惠，这将一项利润收入来源推向中东铁路公司，反而损害了中国政府机构即中国邮政局的利益。为使海关相信自满洲里发寄的邮递包裹确实从中国转运至美国，邮务长提出将包裹置于密封口袋，再运送至上海，并许诺向海关提供复出口凭单，凭单外形与在上海邮政局值班的海关帮办签发的证书一致。邮务长还谈及海关给以货运方式运送的货物退还税款不会带来任何收益，但邮政局那边就要损失一大笔收入了。

李齐先生的观点很合理，从中国政府利益出发，的确值得考虑。他提议向海关提供货物复出口凭单这种方式也很妥当。若海关总税务司愿意重新考虑其决定，准予此种退税优惠，本署没有异议。

您忠诚的仆人

（签字）贾韦（R. C. L. d'Anjou）

哈尔滨关税务司

哈尔滨关致海关总税务司署第2581号呈附件

致哈尔滨关征税汇办处第81号函　　　　　　　哈尔滨邮政局1922年1月6日

尊敬的哈尔滨关税务司：

1. 贵署12月31日第1347号函收悉：

"关于自俄赤塔经中国满洲里复出口到美国的转口皮草退税遭拒一事。"

现答复如下，恳请贵署将以下因素呈请海关总税务司考虑。

2. 自赤塔进口至满洲里，又照联运提单原封不动以货运方式复出口至大连关，再经大连关运往美国的转口货物，尤其是转口皮草，哈尔滨关在收到大连关税务司出具的"复出口凭单"（海关表C–57），证明货物确实"已装船"运往美国后，海关允许给予退税。

3. 我确信，凡在满洲里发寄的原装皮草（即原包装完整，未拆封），倘若从满洲里用密封包裹邮件寄送到上海市中国邮政局，经过派驻在该局、负责包裹征税的海关帮办证明，它们确实"已装船"运往美国，那么该货物有资格享受与可退税皮草相同的海关退税优惠待遇。需要强调的是，那些可退税皮草的运费是支付给一家不会给中国政府增加收入的公司。如贵署所知，若这些皮草包裹在中国发寄，使用密封邮件经满洲里转运到美国，就不会牵扯中国海关征税办法的问题了。

4. 对按照联运提单以货运方式运送的货物给予退税，但对邮递包裹方式不给予同种优惠，这将会促使货物涌向日本铁路运输，导致中国政府无法从此高利润业务中分一杯羹，丧失大笔邮资收入；而对联运提单货运方式转口货物恢复退税办法，海关实则不会获得任何利润。满洲里东三省有两家大宗皮货商人此刻准备寄运一大批货物，正在等待包裹邮寄货物退税问题的决定。如果中国邮政局承运的货物与其他国家部门受到的待遇不一致，他们则会考虑走货运方式（如由日本铁路运至大连再由日本轮船运至美国）。

5. 美国总领事也就包裹邮寄皮草一事向本署致函，等收到贵署回函结果后，本署再向美国总领事答复。

6. 此事事关邮政管理局收入，恳请贵署在此事上给予支持。

您忠诚的仆人

（签字）李齐（W.W.Ritchie）

北满洲邮政司

10. 为按照满洲特别免重征执照或其他凭单进口后又需再复出口到国外的土货征税办法事

85.

I. G.

Aigun/Taheiho 9th December, 1922.

監去第九十二号

監來第三百X号

Sir,

I have the honour to append copy of a despatch received from the Superintendent, reporting certain grievances of the Chamber of Commerce against the Customs, and of my reply thereto.

The original letter of the Chamber complains that the Customs do not allow free re-exportation abroad of native goods arrived in Aigun Taheiho by the overland route, under Transit Pass, and states that only goods covered by Harbin Duty Receipt are re-exported free of duty.

The facts are these : not many days ago, a case was brought to my notice, of native cargo being applied for Blagovestchensk, said to have arrived under Manchurian Special E.C., but without any marks

or

The Inspector General of Customs.

Peking.

or numbers on the Import and Re-export Applications. I directed that duty be charged. - However, not more than a week later, before the question had been raised by the merchants, I found out that it had been the consistent practice here to accept Re-export Applications without marks, on the strength of a Document such as an E. C., Manchurian Special E. C., etc, and to pass without payment of duty such native goods when sent to Blagovestchensk: although this practice appeared to me as entirely wrong, and detrimental to the Revenue, I gave orders to revert to it, pending reference of this point to you. Very few cases therefore occurred, in which free re-exportation was refused. - The Chinese Chamber of Commerce evidently mistakes Manchurian Sp. E. C. for Transit Pass; and they are entirely wrong in saying that we only allow native goods to be re-exported abroad free of duty, if they are covered by Harbin Duty Receipt.

I now have the Honour to solicit your sanction to a change in the practice of this Office, so as to bring it into line with rules observed anywhere else; i.e. that free re-exportation abroad of native goods imported under any document' only be

allowed

allowed if the cargo is properly identifiable, by means of marks affixed to the packing, and entered on the documents, the Import and Re-export Applications.

The Handbook for Customs Procedure at Shanghai, under the heading "Re-export Cargo", states that N. E. O.s and drawbacks on native goods re-exported abroad are granted on condition "that the goods remain intact in their original packages with their original marks unchanged", and it is clear that, in the absence of marks, identification is practically impossible.

The loss to the Revenue through the wrong practice in force here for several years is considerable for this Port: now that we have given way in the matter of taxation of overland native cargo, we should, in my opinion, be very strict on other points.

The Superintendent is informed, in my reply, that I am asking you to alter the practice existing at Aigun Taheiho; I have also called his attention, verbally, to the incorrect and impolite language of the Chamber, and he has warned the Chamber to use in future more considerate words, when writing to, or about, Government Officials and Offices.

I have, etc.

J. Bock

Acting Commissioner.

[A.—27 e]

No. 104 Commrs.

Inspectorate General of Customs,

Aigun No. 92,886 PEKING, 26th January, 1923.

SIR,

I am directed by the Inspector General to acknowledge receipt of your Despatch No. 85 :

Native Goods imported under Manchurian Special Exemption Certificate or other document, re-exported abroad, granted, by local practice, duty free treatment even if not properly identifiable, reporting. Authority to alter existing practice soliciting;

and, in reply, to state as follows :

1. The facts of the particular case to which you refer, i.e. of Native cargo being applied for,- for export to Blagovestchensk - " said to have arrived under Special Manchurian Exemption Certificate, but without any marks or numbers on the import and re-export applications", are not clear; for you have not given information on the following points : Where did the goods arrive

The Commissioner of Customs,

A I G U N.

arrive from ? By what office was the Special Manchurian Exemption Certificate supposed to have been issued? Was the Special Manchurian Exemption Certificate not presented for inspection? If not presented, was it called for by the Customs ? This document should, of course, contain marks, numbers, and description of the packages which it covers: as the applications did not contain these particulars, was the applicant called on to " correct " the applications ? Was any attempt made by the Customs to identify the goods ?

2. It has long been the practice in the Harbin Customs district - to which your office originally belonged - to free native goods covered by a Special Manchurian Exemption Certificate from further duty on exportation, upon satisfactory identification of the goods with those for which the document was originally granted. Although this practice was established without definite authority, the Inspector General,

when

when it was reported to him, did not disallow its continuance, but he pointed out that a Special Manchurian Exemption Certificate was issued for the special purpose of freeing goods from inland taxation within the confines of Manchuria and its use for any other purpose could not be claimed; and that therefore each case should be judged on its merits.

3. The documents covering the cargo should, of course, be presented for inspection, and satisfactory identification of the cargo as that which has already paid Customs duties is of course necessary; but the document to be inspected for purposes of identification is the Special Manchurian Exemption Certificate - which should contain all the necessary particulars for that purpose - and not the application. You do not state that the merchants object to such identification of their cargo, and it should not be difficult to arrange with them that their

applications

applications should contain the necessary particulars. If the Special Manchurian Exemption Certificate does not contain the necessary particulars as regards marks and numbers, etc. you should refer to the issuing office.

4. Before making any change in existing practice you are requested to report further on the matter, describing in detail what that practice is, and giving information on the points referred to in §1 of this despatch both with regard to the particular case mentioned and with regard to other cases, with special reference to the documents covering the cargo, the offices by which these documents were issued, and the routes by which the cargo arrived.

I am,

Sir,

Your obedient Servant,

Cecil A. V. Bowra,

Chief Secretary.

96

I. G. Aigun / Taheiho 23rd February, 23

Sir,

I have the honour to acknowledge the receipt of your despatch No. 104/92,886 (in reply to Aigun despatch No. 85):

Native cargo imported under Manchurian Special Exemption Certificate or other document, subsequently re-exported abroad : duty treatment of : further report called for:

and to reply as follows.

1. This Office, according to practice of the Harbin Office, has always passed free of duty on re-exportation abroad native goods having already paid duty at the Maritime Customs, whether imported under Manchurian Special Exemption Certificate or other document.

2. Goods are originally imported

a) under duplicate Export Application, from Harbin during the navigation season

b) under Manchurian Special Exemption Certificate

or

The Inspector General of Customs,

P E K I N G.

or Special Exemption Certificate (for Factory Products), exceptionally under Yümtan or P'ing-tan, from Harbin, Dairen and Newchwang, in summer or winter, by River or Overland.

3. Duplicate Export Applications covering goods from Harbin often do not bear marks; Manchurian Special Exemption Certificates issued by the Harbin and Dairen Offices not infrequently bear no marks or numbers; Newchwang invariably gives marks and full particulars on Manchurian Special Exemption Certificates, and numbers are seldom given by any issuing Office.

4. This Office has failed in several instances to send back for correction the Manchurian Special Exemption Certificate bearing no marks or numbers; an excuse for this may be found in the fact that the Aigun Office has never issued such documents, and that some of the goods they cover, very difficult to mark by their packing (hemp rope in hanks, copper and galvanised iron wire in coils), lead to the belief that the marks and numbers may be dispensed with in certain cases.

5.

5. On arrival of native as well as foreign goods, goods are usually checked, documents are invariably called out for inspection, and the marks and numbers, if any, entered on the Import Application.

6. If goods are re-exported at once, the original document can be consulted; if they are re-exported some time after importation (within a year), importation can only be traced by means of the Import Application.

7. On re-exportation, goods are carefully checked with the original Import Application, and, if found in order as regards quality and quantity, are passed free, irrespective of marks and numbers.

8. The particular case referred to in my despatch No. 16 was that of native sheeting declared for re-exportation to Blagoveschensk; the Application stated that the goods had been imported from Dairen under Manchurian Special Exemption Certificate, and reference to the Import Application showed this to be the case; but neither the Import nor the Re-export Application had indication of marks or numbers. The applicant

thereupon

thereupon withdrew his application.

9. By referring all Manchurian Special Exemption Certificates without marks and numbers to the issuing Office, the question of re-exportation of native goods covered by such documents will be easily eliminated; but goods originally imported from Harbin under duplicate Application may have no marks, and in such case the practice of this Office should in my opinion, be altered, so that only such goods as are strictly identifiable (i.e. with marks and numbers unchanged) be granted free export privileges.

I beg therefore to solicit your instructions in the matter; in order to avoid difficulties with merchants, the new correct practice may be made to apply only to goods imported after receipt of your decision.

Copy of this despatch is being forwarded to the Harbin Commissioner.

I have the honour to be,

Sir,

Your obedient Servant,

G. Zochi

Acting Commissioner.

[A.—27 c]

No. 109 Commrs.

Aigun No. 93,410

Inspectorate General of Customs,

PEKING, 13th March 1923.

SIR,

I am directed by the Inspector General to acknowledge receipt of your Despatch No. 96 (with reference to your despatch No. 85 and I. G. despatch No. 104/92,886):

Cargo, Native: imported under Special Manchurian Exemption Certificate or other document and subsequently re-exported abroad: duty treatment re:

and, in reply, to say that your view that only such duty-paid goods as are strictly identifiable should be granted free re-export privileges is undoubtedly correct. But, as it would appear that difficulties in the way of identification by your office arise from the fact that in some cases the necessary particulars (marks, numbers etc.) are not duly entered on the covering documents issued by other Custom

Houses,

THE COMMISSIONER OF CUSTOMS,

A I G U N.

Houses, you should call the attention of the offices concerned to these omissions, and request them to enter on the documents issued by them all necessary particulars for the proper identification of cargo. When this has been done and time allowed for it to have proper effect, you should inform merchants that in future free re-export privileges can be granted only to such goods as are properly identifiable as those covered by the relative documents.

The Harbin practice, as reported in Harbin No. 2810, appears to conform to the above principle.

A copy of this despatch is being sent to the Harbin Commissioner.

I am,

Sir,

Your obedient Servant,

L. de Luca,

Chief Secretary.

呈海关总税务司署 85 号文　　瑷珲关 / 大黑河 1922 年 12 月 9 日

尊敬的海关总税务司(北京):

随呈附上海关监督与本署就商会对海关提出不满一事的往来信函抄件(监来字第三百零七号及监去字第九十三号)。

商会于来函中抱怨称,瑷珲关对于持子口税票经陆路运抵瑷珲 / 大黑河后复出口至国外的土货未予免税放行,仅允许持有哈尔滨关完税收据者免税复出口至国外。

事实上,不久之前,确有一批自称持有满洲特别免重征执照的土货申请复出口至布拉戈维申斯克(Blagovestchensk),但因其进口及复出口报单中均无任何标记或编号,本署遂命令予以征税。但之后不到一周,便有商人前来对此次征税提出质疑。随后本署才发现,按照本关惯例,凡土货持有免重征执照或满洲特别免重征执照等凭证者,复出口时报单上若无标记,亦可免税复出口至布拉戈维申斯克。本署虽认为此惯例完全错误,且有损税收,但已于等待贵署指令期间,下令予以恢复。自此,免税复出口遭到拒绝之事鲜有发生。显然,中国商会是误将满洲特别免重征执照当成子口税票,其关于瑷珲关仅允许持有哈尔滨关完税收据之土货免税复出口至国外之言论亦完全错误。

兹请求批准瑷珲关更改此惯例,与他口规章保持一致,即凡持海关凭证进口后申请免税复出口至国外之土货,唯有可通过外包装上,海关凭证内以及进口和复出口报单内之标记识别者,方可获准。

《海关实务手册》(*The Handbook for procedure at shanghai*)中“复出口货物”部分已载明,凡复出口至国外之土货,“唯完整存于原包装内,且包装上的原标记无更改”者,方允许退税。显然,若无标记,货物难以识别。

本口因实施该项错误惯例多年,已造成巨额税收损失,如今既已于土货陆路运输征税一事上做出让步,其他方面更应严格把控。

本署已回函告知海关监督向贵署申请修改惯例一事,亦口头请其注意商会之错误及无礼措辞;海关监督已警告商会今后信函无论是发与政府官员和机构,还是内容与之有关,均须谨慎用词。

您忠诚的仆人

包安济(G. Boezi)

瑷珲关署理税务司

致瑷珲关第104/92886号令　　　　海关总税务司署(北京)1923年1月26日

尊敬的瑷珲关税务司:

第85号呈收悉:

"汇报如下情况:凡按照满洲特别免重征执照或其他凭单进口之后、又需再复出口到国外的土货,根据当地惯例,即便其出处不太好辨认,一律予以免税放行。请示改变现有做法。"

奉总税务司命令,现批复如下:

1. 贵署所提及的特例,即报运出口的土货(比如出口到布拉格维申斯克)的信息不清楚,"据称其已遵照满洲特别免重征执照的规定抵达关区,但进口报单和复出口报单上均没有任何标记或序号";因为贵署并没有针对以下要点给出相关信息:这些货物来自何处?满洲特别免重征执照是由何处签发?是否出示满洲特别免重征执照请求检验?如未出示,海关是否要求出示?此凭单应包括标记、序号及商品件数描述:若报单中不包括上述细节,是否要求报关人"纠正"报单内容?海关是否进行了货物鉴定尝试?

2. 长久以来,哈尔滨关区(原来为贵署的上级机构)一直遵循的做法是:凡满洲特别免重征执照所涵盖的土货,一经鉴定为遵循执照报关的货物,则予以免税复出口。虽然此惯例的确立并没有得到明确的授权,但上报总税务司后,其并没有禁止这一行为,而是指出,之所以签发满洲特别免重征执照,是为了免除满洲境内货物的内地统捐,且不得用于其他目的;因此每个案件都应按实情判定。

3. 上述载明货物的凭单应当出示报验,便于正确鉴定完税货物;在这种情况下,用于货物鉴定的报验凭单不应是报单,而是满洲特别免重征执照。为实现鉴定目的,该执照应包含所有必要的细节。贵署并没有说明商人们是否反对上述货物鉴定。请与商人商定报单内应包含的细节,我想完成这件事应当不太困难。若满洲特别免重征执照没有包括必要的细节,例如标记或序号等,贵署应向发照机构提交修改意见。

4. 在对现行惯例做出更改前,贵署应汇报关于此问题的更多信息,详细描述现行惯例是什么,提供此文中第一条所提及的信息,并且务必注明货物凭单、凭单签发机构及货物运抵路线。

您忠诚的仆人

包罗(C. A. V. Bowra)

总务科税务司

呈海关总税务司署96号文　　　　　　　瑷珲关/大黑河1923年2月23日

尊敬的海关总税务司（北京）：

根据海关总税务司署第104/92886号令（回复瑷珲关第85号呈）：

“请进一步汇报瑷珲关对持有满洲特别免重征执照或其他海关凭证进口后申请复出口至国外之土货的征税办法。”

兹回复如下：

1. 根据哈尔滨关惯例，凡土货已于海关完纳税款并持有满洲特别免重征执照或其他海关凭证进口者，复出口至国外时，瑷珲关均予免税放行。

2. 货物最初进口时：

1）若于航运季自哈尔滨关进口，通常持有出口报单副本；

2）若于夏季或冬季经由水运或陆路自哈尔滨关、大连关、牛庄关进口，通常持有满洲特别免重征执照或特别免重征执照（工厂产品特有），亦有持有运单或凭单者。

3. 自哈尔滨关进口之货物所持出口报单副本上常无标记；哈尔滨关及大连关签发之满洲特别免重征执照常无标记或编号；牛庄关签发之满洲特别免重征执照一直附带标记，并载有货物详情；各关所签发之满洲特别免重征执照皆鲜有编号。

4. 此前遇有满洲特别免重征执照上无标记或编号者，本关曾多次退还纠正未果；其中缘由或因本关从未签发过此照，或因有些货物之包装难以标记（如成卷麻绳、铜线及镀锌线等），以致各关以为于某些情况下可免除标记及编号。

5. 凡货物运抵后，无论土洋，本关均会予以查验，并检查相关凭证，如有标记及编号，均会登记在进口报单上。

6. 若货物立即复出口，则可通过其原始凭证了解进口信息；若货物于进口一段时日后复出口（一年内），则只能通过进口报单调查其进口信息。

7. 凡货物申请复出口者，本关均会按原进口报单仔细核对，经查质量与数量均无改变后，无论有无标记和编号，均予免税放行。

8. 瑷珲关第85号呈所提案例具体情况为，有一批土产床单布申请复出口至布拉戈维申斯克，并于复出口报单中载明货物自大连关进口且持有满洲特别免重征执照，而其进口报单信息亦与之相符；但无论是进口报单或是复出口报单皆无标记或编号，商人遂撤回其申报。

9. 兹建议，凡满洲特别免重征执照未附标记及编号者，均应直接退还签发各关查证，以解决持此照复出口之土货的相关问题；此外，对于自哈尔滨关进口，但所持出口报单副本无标记之货物，亦应规定，唯有清晰可辨者（即标记及编号无更改），方可享有免税出口之特权。

特此申请批准上述建议，以避免与商人有何冲突，在收到贵署指令前，本署将继续照现行惯例行事。

此抄件发送至哈尔滨关税务司。

您忠诚的仆人

包安济（G. Boezi）

瑷珲关署理税务司

致瑷珲关第 109/93410 号令　　　　海关总税务司署(北京)1923 年 3 月 13 日

尊敬的瑷珲关税务司:

第 96 号呈收悉:(根据贵署第 85 号呈及海关总税务司署第 104/92886 号令):

"按照满洲特别免重征执照或其他凭单进口之后,又需再复出口到国外的土货的征税办法。"

奉总税务司命令,现批复如下:兹告知,只有那些经过严格查验鉴定为完税的货物才应给予免税复出口特权,您的这一观点完全正确。然而,在某些情况下,其他海关颁发的凭单并没有登记必要的细节(如完税标记、序号等),这会给贵署的货物鉴定工作带来很大困难,您应当向相关海关反映此类遗漏问题,并要求其在凭单上登记所有必要的细节,便于对货物进行鉴定。贵署完成此事后,在规定生效之前为商人留出一定的过渡期,并告知商人,将来只有经查验鉴定为凭单所载之物的货物才能享有免税复出口的特权。

如哈尔滨关第 2810 号呈报告所示,哈尔滨关的做法与上述原则相符。

同时,此令副本已抄送给哈尔滨关税务司。

您忠诚的仆人

包罗(C. A. V. Bowra)

总务科税务司

11. 为汇报乘客所携行李及船员所携包裹中应税物品的征税惯例事

94.

I. G. Aigun / Taheiho 7th February, 3.

Sir,

In accordance with the instructions of your Circular No. 3372, II :

Dutiable articles carried in passengers' luggage and dutiable parcels carried by steamers employes : report re, called for;

I have the honour to report that the present practice at this Port, for which no special authority could be quoted, is as follows :

1. The amount of duty collectible from any one person, which, if not exceeded, is not collected, is about $ 1.00.

2. At Taheiho no duty is collected on board vessels: dutiable articles of $ 20.00 or over in value, either entered on the manifest (luggage list or parcel list), or declared verbally by the passengers or members of the crew

a) if the steamer is entering Port, are handed to the Second Mate for custody, until they can be escorted to the Custom House, where they are made

The Inspector General of Customs,

P E K I N G.

made to pay duty;

b) if the steamer is clearing, are sent to the Custom House to pay Duty, unless the steamer's clearance is too much delayed thereby in which case the articles are shut-out.

3. At Aigun, such articles are occasionally allowed to pay duty on board; steamers, in fact, often make a very short stay in Aigun, and, there being only one responsible Officer at that Station, while he boards a vessel, there is no Employé empowered to collect duties in the Office.

4. Dutiable goods of a value of $ 20.00 or over, if undeclared, are seized and dealt with according to circumstances.

I would only propose a few changes to the present practice. - I do not deem it expedient to have duties collected on board at Taheiho : the rush of work and shortage of Staff often compel this Office to put very junior Officers in charge of Boarding Parties, and they should not be given additional work and responsibility; besides, this Port is small, and the distance from any vessel to the Custom House is insignificant, so that there is little inconvenience and great advantage in having all duties paid in the General Office. - The verbal declarations from <u>bona fide</u> passengers should be accepted as

before

before, but steamer employés should be made to enter any parcel carried by them on the Manifest, under penalty of confiscation. - The amount of duty which, if not exceeded, need not be collected, should, in my opinion, be fixed at $ 0.50.

I have the honour to be,

Sir,

Your obedient Servant,

J. Bolch

Acting Commissioner.

呈海关总税务司署 94 号文　　瑷珲关 / 大黑河 1923 年 2 月 7 日

尊敬的海关总税务司（北京）：

根据海关总税务司署第 3372 号通令（第二辑）：

"请汇报乘客所携行李及船员所携包裹中应税物品的征税办法。"

兹报告，瑷珲关现行惯例如下（无专门授权可引用）：

1. 每人交税金额约为 1.00 银圆，若未超过限额，则不予征税。

2. 大黑河口岸暂无登船征税之例；凡乘客或船员所携物品价值为 20 银圆及以上者，无论是持舱口单（行李单或包裹单）或是口头申报：

1）待轮船入港后，均须暂由轮船二副监管，再由关员护送至海关交税；

2）待轮船清关时，均须送海关交税，因轮船清关延误而短装之货物除外。

3. 瑷珲口岸偶有允许此类物品于船上交税之例；事实上，轮船于瑷珲口岸停留时间通常较短，而该口负责关员仅有一名，若其登船检查，本关内则再无有权征税之人。

4. 凡乘客或船员所携物品价值为 20 银圆及以上者，均须交税，凡未如实申报者，即行查获，并酌情处置。

对于此现行惯例，兹认为，需要稍作调整：仍照常允许乘客口头申报，但船员须为其所携包裹出示舱口单，凡未能照办者，均予罚没；此外，每人交税金额应调整为 0.50 银圆，若未超过 20 银圆限额，则不予征税。然于大黑河口岸而言，登船征税确有不便之处，毕竟此口岸工作繁忙、人手紧缺，凡遇有登船检查之事，往往需要初等关员负责，但此等额外工作和责任实不应强加于其；此外，此口岸较小，船只入港后与海关办公楼的距离都很近，至征税汇办处[①]交税可谓十分便利。

您忠诚的仆人

包安济（G. Boezi）

瑷珲关署理税务司

① 英文为 General Office，1921–1929 年被称为征税汇办处，1929 年后被称为总务课，为海关征税部门，设于海关办公楼内。

12. 为告知拟在中国实施统一的海陆征税办法及需报告采纳上述办法可能产生的贸易后果事

[A.—29]

No. 132 COMMRS.

Aigun No. 94,703

INSPECTORATE GENERAL OF CUSTOMS,

PEKING, 15th June 1923.

Replied to in No. 130.

Sir,

I append, for your information and guidance, copy of Shui-wu Ch'u despatch No. 846, from which you will see that the Preparatory Commission for the Special Conference to be held in Peking in accordance with Article II of the Treaty relating to the Chinese Customs Tariff, concluded at the Washington Conference, wishes to have the views of the Commissioners at the ports concerned as to the possible consequences affecting trade that may result if the principle of uniformity in the rates of Customs duties levied at all the land and maritime frontiers of China, as recognised in Article VI of the above Treaty, is put into force, and

the

The Commissioner of Customs,

AIGUN.

Entered in Card-Index.

the possible remedial measures that may be adopted in case trade were adversely affected by the change, or retaliatory measures were adopted by the foreign powers concerned.

I have accordingly to request you to report as fully as possible on the matter as it affects your port.

Your report is to be accompanied by a Chinese version in duplicate.

I am,

Sir,

Your obedient Servant,

Cecil A. V. Bowra

Officiating Inspector General,

ad interim.

Appendix.

Appendix.

I. G. despatch No. 132 to Aigun.

稅務處令第八四六號

中華民國十二年六月九日

案准外交部關稅特別會議籌備處函開查中國陸路邊界通商貨稅減免辦法曾於中俄條約暨陸路通商章程中英緬甸條約中法滇越通商條約分別載明揆當日立約之意無非爲運輸不便貿易較微故特定此項減免辦法以示體恤今則除緬甸外餘皆交通發達商務繁興遠非昔日所可比擬是以前年中俄商約施行期限屆滿之時政府已毅然先將中俄邊界貿易減免貨稅辦法宣言廢棄惟中東鐵路合同內所規定者現尚照行日本則以要求利益均沾之故所有經由安東暨接近朝鮮間島琿春等處陸路之貨物其進出口稅今亦仍照三分減一交納迨華府會議討論中國關稅條約之時英國代表雖有廢除陸路減稅辦法如一律適用於各邊界則英國亦可承認之宣言而法國代表則仍欲維持滇越邊界貿易之舊制爭之甚力遂於華府會議所訂中國關稅條約之第六條一面承認海陸各邊界劃一徵稅之原則仍一面聲明凡遇交換某種局部經濟利益會許以關稅之特權者應於取消該特權之際由特別會議秉公調劑之竊思此項減免貨稅辦法就原

則而言中國自應趁此時機實行廢棄以使海陸徵稅辦法歸於一律惟減免貨稅制度一經廢除則中國商人因條約關係所享之互惠條件亦必同時取消當華府會議時英國代表已有此項之聲明倘照此實行則滇桂邊關貨稅固可免去減徵之損失而土貨之運往緬越者當亦深受其影響矧吾國之滇桂各處貨物經由越南而轉運至沿海各口者於通過法境時亦不能再受低率征稅之利雖華會條約載有特別會議得爲秉公調劑之明文惟應以何法能爲公平之調劑並能調劑至若何地步此則純係事實問題非可預爲懸揣者擬請貴處令行總稅務司分別轉飭各關係稅務司迅將中俄中日中英中法各邊界貿易情形詳細查明具復並由各該稅司體察當地情形對於減免貨稅取消之後將生如何影響暨應如何補救之處儘可各抒所見俾本處獲收集思廣益之效應函達查照辦理見復等因前來相應令行代理總稅務司查照轉令中英中法中俄中韓邊界各關稅務司遵照前開事理詳議具復再由總稅務司審核擬具意見呈復本處以憑核轉可也此令

趙桂山
周啓明 同校

致瑷珲关第132/94703号令　　　　海关总税务司署（北京）1923年6月15日

尊敬的瑷珲关税务司：

为了便于贵署顺利执行，兹附税务处第846号令副本，以供参考。据该令所示，根据华盛顿会议签订条约第二条关于中国关税方面的内容，拟在北京召开外交部关税特别会议。该会议筹备处现希望征询各相关口岸税务司关于下列问题的意见：如果中国按照条约第四条实施统一的海陆征税办法将会给贸易带来何种影响；为了应对上述变化所带来的不利贸易影响，或者应对外国采取的报复性措施，应当采取哪些补救措施。

据此，由于此令关系到贵口岸，贵署应尽可能就此事做一份全面的报告。

贵署报告需一式两份，附中文版。

您忠诚的仆人

包罗（C. A. V. Bowra）

代理海关总税务司

13. 为汇报俄国当局拒不承认道尹所签发的过境小票及道尹对俄方实施贸易封锁事

TAHEIHO-BLAGOVESTCHENSK TRAFFIC: refusal of russian authorities to recognise Taoyin's frontier passes; establishment of commercial blockade; commissioner's attitude & action taken, reporting: remarks.

Aigun 13th. July 3

Replied to in No. 140.

Sir,

1. The refusal of the russian authorities at Blagovestchensk to recognise frontier passes (小票) issued by the Hei Ho Taoyin has provoked a retaliator spirit on the part of the chinese and communication between Taheiho and Blagovestchensk has come to a standstill. The ferry service has ceased to function and a commercial blockade has been established by the chinese authorities with the idea of preventing the entry into or egress from russian territory of cargo of all description.

2. The Taoyin had been in the habit of charging a fee of 21 cents for each frontier pass (小票) issued at his office, but early last month the russian authorities at Blagovestchensk contested his right to issue these passes and notified him that in future people who desired to cross from Taheiho to Blagovestchensk would have to apply for permission to do so to the russian representative at Taheiho who would be authorised to issue " Ta Chao " (大照) good for one month and costing $5.80, and " Hsiao P'iao " (小票), good for one trip only and costing $0.75. The Taoyin replied that he would never

The Inspector General of Customs,

Peking.

Entered in Card-Index.

never agree to a proposal which usurped his authority and after a great deal of discussion the russian authorities offered to reduce the price of a "Ta Chao" (大照) from $5.80 to $3.30 and to make it valid for a period of three months instead of one month. They also expressed willingness to recognise frontier passes issued by the Taoyin on the condition that all such passes were presented at their representative's office for endorsement. They made it clear that they were unable to give way on this point; that without a russian visa passengers would not be allowed to land at Blagovestchensk; and that a fee of $0.22 would be charged for each visa granted.

3. The chinese argue that ninety per cent of the passengers who journey between Taheiho and Blagovestchensk are chinese citizens and that if the russian authorities are permitted to exact toll in this manner money will fructify at a prodigious pace in the pockets of the russian representative whose salary would be paid, and office establishment maintained, out of charitable donations received from chinese sources. They see no reason why chinese savings should provide the capital necessary for a russian "consulate" and declare that they will never allow the russians - ch'iung tang (窮黨) as they are called in this district - to affix their liabilities on chinese shoulders.

4. The Taoyin informed me that it was only after

after the most patient efforts to avoid a rupture that he had been compelled to break with the russian authorities and asked me to note that all cargo, whether chinese- or foreign-owned, should be equally prevented from reaching Blagovestchensk. I submitted that a blockade of the frontier was international in its nature and urged that the pooposal to stop foreign-owned cargo from entering Blagovestchensk took no account of deeper issues and the solid and permanent interests of nationals of the various treaty powers. The Taoyin replied that he had no thought of repudiating, or in any way evading, treaty obligations, but said that in his opinion the matter was entirely an affair of the local authorities. Subsequently he appeared to show some signs of apprehension at the situation and told me that he had wired to the Shui-wu Ch'u for approval of his action. Since despatching this telegram he would seem to have succeeded in suppressing any qualms of conscience he may have experienced and to have come to the conclusion that the safest thing for him to do is to " shout with the largest crowd."

5. The Taoyin, who is also Customs Superintendent and Chiao She Yuan, may be presumed to have no principles but the promotion of his own political career. I understand that there has been a pounding, grinding, unceasing effort on

the

the part of the Chamber of Commerce to weaken him with the people and drive him into submission to their own schemes and plans and he doubtless finds himself in a rather uncomfortable position. He knows, of course, on which side his bread is buttered and since the blockade has been sanctioned by the highest authority in the province it would be political suicide for him to run counter to the wishes of the community. He is consequently doing his best to take himself as much as possible out of the picture and is allowing the matter to stand over in the hope that the course of events may solve the question for him. The mob appears to be under every semblance of discipline, but a noisy minority has been worked up to a state of violent hatred towards russians, and given the opportunity these passionate patriots may be expected to become increasingly intractable and truculent. In a comparatively small place like Taheiho a firm hand could easily keep unruly elements in order, but the Taoyin seems afraid that demonstrations may take a more sinister form and practically admits that he is being forced to play as strong an anti-russian hand as possible.

A society styled " Ching Chi Lien Ho Hui " (經濟聯合會) has been formed locally by the Chinese Chamber of Commerce to deal with this russian question. Meetings are held as a rule in the chamber of commerce hall, but the local

theatre

theatre also provides a forum where crowds meet and expound their views under the guidance of specially appointed lecturers, and there is no doubt that these latter, with their ignorance of customs procedure, their indifference to any opinion which does not coincide with their own, and their impassioned addresses full of fluid ambiguities and misstatements -a few nights ago the lecturer for the evening announced to his audience that, notwithstanding a technical difficulty, the customs had received instructions from the Shui-wu Ch'u to confiscate the cargo brought into port by the russian s.s. " Blagovestchensk " (Vide §8) - have been helping greatly to create a challenging situation. The evident intention is to extend this anti-russian movement on a sympathetic basis throughout Manchuria and in a pamphlet recently issued - a veritable litany of grievances - the Ching Chi Lien Ho Hui (經濟聯合會),who would seem to claim that their transcendent regard for their country has empowered them to take control of every body else's business into their own hands and punish any who contest the propriety of this piece of presumption -two shops have recently been fined $200 each for supplying russian steamers with cargo- have played up to the local public the refusal of the russian authorities to recognise the Taoyin's passes as part of a vast plot against China, fitting it in a circumstantial background composed of the massacre of chinese at

Blagovestchensk

Blagovestchensk at the time of the Boxer rebellion when the old town of Aigun was burned to the ground and China's previous difficulties with the former russian government.

7. On the 22nd. June an american who had arrived from Harbin with a consignment of machinery destined for Blagovestchensk complained to me that the chinese police were forcibly preventing him from handling his cargo. The question put to me by this american was a fair one, and a question which under the circumstances he was bound to ask and I was bound to answer. He protested that the right of an american firm to take delivery of innocent merchandise, the lawful property of the said firm, which had paid all customs dues and duties, was established by treaty, and asked me whether this was so or not. I was successful in my effort to secure the attention of the Taoyin to the grave disadvantages under which foreign merchants would labour if offensively discriminated against and the cargo in question was in due course taken by junks across the river.

8. On the 8th. July the Chamber of Commerce informed the Taoyin that the russian steamer "Blagovestchensk", which had been cleared by this office a few days earlier against the wish of the local authorities, was due to arrive in port at any moment with four barges containing firewood and asked him to direct the commissioner to hand

over

over the cargo to them pending settlement of the matter in dispute. The Taoyin sent me the chamber's letter and requested me to give effect to the wishes expressed therein. Verbally he hinted that evil passions were abroad and that the surrender of the firewood might provide a safety valve. He added that refusal on my part would create a great embarrassment for him and that in the event of disturbances persons and property might no longer be safe. I told the Taoyin that I could not accede to his request. I pointed out that I had well-defined duties, with definite rights and responsibilities; that these duties were not laid before me to take or leave in a casual manner and that it was impossible for me to mortgage any one of my legitimate functions. The Taoyin did not like my attitude and after further considering the matter I decided to detain the ship and cargo and refer to you for instructions. I took this course, not because I considered I had any authority to do so, but solely because it seemed to me essential to recognise that we had got well within scent of very serious trouble. The Taoyin had warned me several times that release of the cargo would be certain to cause a display of violent disorder, but he did not like the idea of seizing it himself, and his reluctance to take this extreme step - a violation of the fundamental law of fair play - both hampered and embarrassed me

because

because it sought to paralyse my powers of resistance and tended to place me in a position in which I would have to accept responsibility for any trouble that might arise. I was thus in every respect at a disadvantage and it was the feeling that, after release of the cargo by the customs, the Taoyin would probably strike an attitude of statuesque inaction, and my desire to free myself from this handicap, that caused me to take a long view of the situation. I submit it was imperative that every possible care should be taken to avoid ugly surprises and make potential danger impossible or negligibly remote, and the only way I could see of doing this was by detaining the firewood pending receipt of your instructions. Your reply to my Telegram of 8th. July was received on the 12th. July and your instructions, which have formed the basis of my argument from the very start, have been given effect to. I shall hardly be expected to disobey an order from my official chief and my position, in consequence, is now no longer so difficult as it was before.

9. It is not possible to say how long this state of affairs is going to last and it would be idle to ignore the fact that wide-spread feelings of ill-will exist on the part of the chinese towards the russians. At the present time, neither side shows any disposition to give way,

but

but trade cannot flourish in a perpetual atmosphere of political rancour and excitement and both sides have a strong inducement to come to a settlement. I think that, taken apart, nine out of ten of the chinese who have business interests here would probably confess in secret that they have no objection to the payment of a small fee to the russian representative for endorsement of passports, and that they are adopting their present attitude because they want to protect themselves and their families from molestation. The ferry, a combination of chinese and russian business interests, is so closely linked with the every day life of the people on both sides of the river, that its place in the local social system can not possibly be overrated. It is the recognised method of transport for both passengers and goods and the interruption to the normal flow of business is so irksome, and is having such a disastrous effect on mutual trade interests from the economic, practical and every point of view that some give-and-take-measures will have to be adopted before long. The local authorities profess to require full and unconditional compliance with their demand that frontier passes should be recognised as valid without endorsement by the russian representative at Taheiho, but it seems reasonable to suppose that they are over-generous in their confidence that it is within their power to dictate arbitrarily

their

their own solution of this matter. Indeed, it is rumoured, and the rumour is credited by reliable persons, though I give the statement with all reserve, that the russians intend to prevent chinese vessels from navigating the Amur.

I have the honour to be,

Sir,

Your obedient Servant,

R. F. C. Hedgeland

Commissioner.

呈海关总税务司署 125 号文　　　　　　　　　　　　瑷珲关 1923 年 7 月 13 日

尊敬的海关总税务司（北京）：

1. 俄布拉戈维申斯克（Blagovestchensk）地区政府拒绝承认黑河道尹所签发的过境小票，中方因此而被激怒并开始实施报复行动，为防止俄国向中国进出口各类货物，中国政府已停止轮渡服务，实施贸易封锁，大黑河与布拉戈维申斯克之间的来往已被阻断。

2. 此前，道尹一直对其签发的过境小票收取 21 分的费用，但本月初，俄布拉戈维申斯克地区政府对道尹是否有权签发此类小票提出质疑，并通知道尹，今后凡自大黑河进入俄布拉戈维申斯克境内之人员，均须向驻大黑河俄国代表申请批准，该俄国代表将会为其签发“大照”或“小票”，“大照”有效期为一个月，每份收费 5.8 银圆，而“小票”仅单次有效，每份收费 0.75 银圆。道尹表示坚决不会同意此等侵权行为。在经过详细讨论之后，俄国政府提出将“大照”的费用从每份 5.8 银圆减至每份 3.3 银圆，并将有效期从一个月增加到三个月；另表示，若道尹签发的过境小票可送至驻大黑河俄国代表办事处获得签字，亦愿承认其效力。但与此同时，俄国政府亦明确表示至此已不会再做让步，凡无俄国签证之人员，将一律无法进入俄布拉戈维申斯克地区，签证费为每次 0.22 银圆。

3. 中方认为，俄布拉戈维申斯克与大黑河之间的往来人员中，百分之九十皆为中国人，若允许俄国政府以此等方式收取过境费，此部分金钱将纳入俄国政府私囊，用以维持俄国代表之薪俸及办公经费。他们认为中国人上交之钱银资助俄国“领事馆”实在毫无道理可言，坚称绝不允许俄国人（大黑河地区民众称之为“穷党”）将债务强加给中国人。

4. 道尹告知本署，其已努力与俄方交涉，但仍无疾而终，最终不得不与之决裂，望海关注意，所有货物，无论土洋，一概不许放行至俄布拉戈维申斯克。本署于回函中表示，封锁边境在性质上属于国际行为，禁止洋货进入俄布拉戈维申斯克之提议实在有欠妥当，亦未考虑到有约各国的长远利益。然道尹回复称其并无否认或逃避条约义务之意，但在其看来，此乃地方政府职权范围内之事务。不过，道尹随后开始理解当前之形势，并告知本署其已向税务处发送电报，申请批准其封锁边境之提议。

5. 黑河道尹（兼海关监督及瑷珲关交涉员）独断专行，毫无原则，仅关心自己仕途升迁之事。据了解，商会方面对道尹一直采取软硬兼施之策，以期动摇其威信，迫使其按照商会的方案与计划行事。道尹当然清楚自己处境艰难，更深知怎样才能巩固其地位，商业封锁既为省政府之命，道尹自不会违背，否则无异于自断前程。正因如此，道尹方会对本署之建议迟迟不予理会，希望能够不了了之，以免牵涉其中。目前，当地商人表面看似安分，但仍有一小部分激进爱国分子对俄方蠢蠢欲动，一旦抓住机会行动起来，便会更加难以压制。大黑河地域较小，即使有不服管制之人，政府亦完全有能力使用强制手段将之镇压，但道尹似乎担心示威之事会愈演愈烈，因此不愿有此等行动，其已承认对俄方采取强硬手段亦属无奈之举。

6. 中国商会已于当地成立“经济联合会”，以应对此次俄国之事；会议通常会于商会会堂召开会议，但有时亦于当地剧院进行召开，由演讲者引导，成员们各抒己见。然而，这些演讲者并不了解海关的工作，遇有不同意见，亦不予理会，只是一味进行着充满激情的演讲，然而内容却往往含糊不清甚至错漏百出，以致事态更加恶化。数日前的一个夜晚，一位演讲者当众说道：“尽管存在一定困难，但海关已收到税务处指令，将没收俄国‘布拉戈维申斯克’号轮船运至大黑河的一切货物。”（参阅第 8 条）此等会议之目的显然是为了引起民众之共鸣，以期将“反俄运动”推向整个满洲。经济联合会于近期发放的宣传册上声称为了国家之利益，举凡涉及贸易之事，均需由其掌控，如有反其道而行者，必会严惩不怠。目前，已有两家商铺因向俄国轮船提供货物而被强制收缴了 200 银圆的罚款。此外，经济联合会还向公众强调，义和团运动时期中国人曾在俄布拉戈维申斯克遭到屠杀[①]，瑷珲旧镇也曾被焚烧殆尽，前俄国政府昔日亦对中国多有刁难，在这样的背景下，俄国当局如今拒绝承认道尹所签发小票之效力，很可能是针对中国而酝酿的又一场阴谋。

7. 6 月 22 日，一名美国人向本署投诉，称其计划从哈尔滨运送一批机械设备至俄布拉戈维申斯克，但却于大黑河遭到中国警方的强行阻拦。对此，其表示根据条约规定，美国公司有权运送合法货物，而这批机械设备乃为公司合法财产，且已完纳应缴费用及税款；并请本署说明是否确应照此办理。其所提问题合乎情理，本署自当予以解决，遂劝说道尹不应贸然歧视洋商，否则后果将会十分严重。该批机械设备最终通过民船及时运送至俄布拉戈维申斯克。

8. 7 月 8 日，商会向道尹汇报称，海关于几日前违背当地政府之意愿，擅自为俄国“布拉戈维申斯克”号轮船办理结关，并说明该轮船携四艘满载薪柴之驳船，随时可能抵港，望其命海关在中俄问题得以解决之前，暂将货物交与商会保管。道尹将商会来函寄与本

---

① 即海兰泡惨案。是 1900 年 7 月 16 日至 21 日沙皇俄国对居住于海兰泡的中国居民进行屠杀的事件，该事件共造成五千多名（也有资料为六七千名）中国人死亡。

署,要求照此办理,并暗示目前群情激愤,若可交出薪柴,或可保安全,另说明若本署拒不照办,必会使其陷入尴尬境地,且一旦发生动乱,人身财产便再无保障。本署向道尹说明实难照办,并指出海关权责明确,一切均须遵照规定执行,无法擅自行动,亦不可将手握之权作为谈判之筹码。道尹对此十分不满,此前已多次警告本署,不可放行这批薪柴,否则必会引起暴乱,但其既不愿亲自接收这批薪柴,亦不想采取任何极端措施。本署因此而陷入两难之境地,既不可放行,又不得不对这批薪柴可能带来的一切麻烦负责,均十分不利。本署虽希望可尽快摆脱当下之困境,但因考虑一旦海关放行这批薪柴,道尹很可能会摆出置之不理之态,故只能从长计议。兹以为,为将潜在风险降至最低,以防事发之时措手不及,唯有暂时收缴这批薪柴,以待贵署指示,方为上策。目前形势严峻,必须确保海关正常运作。海关总税务司署对瑷珲关7月8日电呈之回复已于7月12日收悉,本署已照贵署指示办理,目前之处境已然明朗了许多。

9. 当前状态还要持续多久尚不确定,中国人对俄国人仍有一定的敌对情绪,且双方目前均无妥协之意,但如果长期处于这种因政治斗争而骚动不安的大环境下,贸易实难以发展,为此,中俄双方亦会尽快设法解决此事。兹以为,在大黑河做生意的中国人,十之八九都会暗中表示愿意付给俄方代表一些费用以保证护照的顺利签发,他们之所以表面上仍持有当前这种敌视、对抗之态度,只是为了自己和家人免受骚扰。轮渡将中俄双方的商业利益紧紧捆绑在一起,与华俄两岸人民的日常生活更是密切相关,是当地公认的客运及货运方式,有着举足轻重之地位。轮渡之中断,无论从经济性、实用性或是其他各种角度来说,均会给贸易双方的利益带来灾难性的影响。因此,需要尽快出台互惠互利性质之政策。大黑河地方政府坚持要求俄方无条件服从其要求,承认道尹签发之过境小票即使没有俄国驻大黑河代表之签字亦应具有效力,认为其可以专横独断地解决此事,但其实只是刚愎自用。目前已有传言称俄方意欲禁止中国轮船在黑龙江上航行,一些可靠人士也一致表示该传言属实。

您忠诚的仆人

贺智兰(R. F. C. Hedgeland)

瑷珲关税务司

14. 为瑷珲关区各种货物皆按正税率例征收事

CUSTOMS TARIFFS: full duty charged on all goods in Aigun District, no deductions being allowed. (Enclosure).

130

I.G

Aigun 11th. August 3

Sir,

I have the honour to acknowledge receipt of your Despatch No. 132/94,703 :

CUSTOMS TARIFFS: principle of uniformity in rates levied at land and maritime frontiers of China recognised at Washington Conference. Possible consequences on trade resulting from adoption. Report in re called for;

and, in reply, to submit that the question raised would hardly seem to concern this district where full duty is charged on all goods, no deductions being allowed. The Duty Free List, originally introduced as a temporary measure framed to meet a special set of circumstances which were exceptional at the moment, was abolished in April 1922 and its withdrawal does not appear to have impeded the circulation of commodities or in any way to have injured the interests of trade. Revision of duty rates to meet the changing conditions of the times, as

sanctioned

The Inspector General of Customs,

Peking.

Entered in Card-Index.

sanctioned at the Washington Conference would be fair to China and not unfair to importers; to such a course there can be, generally speaking, no objection in principle, but whether at other frontier ports there are fundamental difficulties of an economic character which it will be hard to avoid I have no means of knowing. In 1919 the Soviet Government not only professed to evince a most sensitive regard towards China, but ostentatiously affected complete indifference to the many privileges extorted by the late Russian Imperial Government, and since the new Russian Tariff, which fully bears out the description of the measure as highly protectionist, has presumably been created for the definite object of restricting trade by Chinese and foreign merchants, any protest on the part of the Soviet against a fair adjustment by China of her tariff would surely be a monstrous proceeding.

2. A Chinese version of this brief report

is

is enclosed in duplicate as directed.

I have the honour to be,

Sir,

Your obedient Servant,

R. F. C. Hedgeland

Commissioner.

Aigun Despatch No. 130 to I.G.

Append No.

為遵令詳查中俄邊界貿易情形具覆事竊查愛琿關各種貨物皆按正稅率例徵收無減稅之辦法與本埠無重要之關係特別免稅辦法實為特別情形而設民國十一年四月取消後與本埠運輸貨物無何項阻碍貿易利益亦無損失中國關稅新定稅則業經華盛頓會議承認與特勢之便遷正合對於中國實為公允而對於進口貨主亦無有不公允之處以此而論無反抗之虞或有他處邊界根本上有所困難之事非所知也查蘇俄政府在民國八年宣言與中國親善關於俄帝國時代所得中國特別利益有全行放棄之表示現蘇俄新定稅則載明各種限制俄人自守之主義以此義推行則中國及他國商業均被限制矣現中國改定邊界稅則而蘇俄如發生反對之事甚可怪異所有遵令調查情形為此呈覆謹呈

總稅務司

愛琿關稅務司賀智蘭

中華民國十二年八月十一日

呈海关总税务司署 130 号文　　　　瑷珲关 1923 年 8 月 11 日

尊敬的海关总税务司（北京）：

根据海关总税务司署第 132/94703 号令：

“关税：华盛顿会议业已承认在中国实施统一海陆征税办法事；请汇报若照此办法征税，对贸易将有何影响。”

兹汇报，瑷珲关各种货物皆按正税率例征收，无减税之办法与本埠无重要之关系。特别免税办法实为特别情形而设，1922 年 4 月取消后，与本埠运输货物无何项阻碍，贸易利益亦无损失。中国关税新定税则业经华盛顿会议承认，正合时势之变迁，对于中国实为公允，而对于进口货主亦无有不公允之处；以此而论，无反抗之虞，或有他处边界根本上有所困难之事，非所知也。查苏俄政府在 1919 年表示与中国亲善，放弃俄帝国时代在中国所得特别利益，现苏俄新定税则载明各种限制俄人自守之主义，以此义推行，则中国及他国商业均被限制矣，现中国改定边界税则，而苏俄如发生反对之事，甚可怪矣。

2. 兹附此简要报告之中文版本，一式两份。

您忠诚的仆人

贺智兰（R. F. C. Hedgeland）

瑷珲关税务司

15. 为呈送 1914—1924 年机制洋式货物及机制面粉出口价值报告事

STATISTICS: value of Chinese factory products exported, value of machine-milled flour exported, and value of revenue stamps affixed to conveyance certificates for period 1914-24, reporting.

239.

I.G.

Aigun 30th. September, 1925.

Sir,

I have the honour to acknowledge receipt of your Circular No. 3641:

Statistics: Ch'u calls for report on value of Chinese factory products exported, value of machine-milled flour exported, and value of revenue stamps affixed to conveyance certificates for period 1914-24;

Appendix. and to hand you herewith the figures called for.

I have the honour to be,

Sir,

Your obedient Servant,

Commissioner.

APPENDIX.

AIGUN NO. 239 TO I. G.

APPENDIX.

(1) Statement showing the total value of Chinese factory products exported abroad from Aigun during each year of the period 1914-1924, both dates inclusive.

NIL.

(2) Statement showing the total value of Chinese factory products exported coastwise from Aigun during each year of the period 1914-1924, both dates inclusive.

NIL.

(3) Statement showing the value of machine-milled flour exported from Aigun abroad and coastwise during each year of the period 1914-1924, both dates inclusive.

1914-1921: These figures are not available. The Aigun Customs was made a charge independent of Harbin from the 1st October, 1921, but the Aigun Returns were rendered by the Harbin Customs until the end of that year. It was from the 1st January 1922 that the Aigun Returns were rendered directly by the Aigun Customs. Vide I. G. No. 1/85,630 to Aigun.

1922:	Hk. Tls.	688,625
1923:	Hk. Tls.	298,789
1924:	Hk. Tls.	150.555

(4)

(4) Statement showing the total value of revenue stamps affixed to conveyance certificates issued by the Aigun Customs to cover machine-milled flour and Chinese factory products during each year of the period 1914-1924, both dates inclusive.

NIL.

Commissioner.

CUSTOM HOUSE,

Aigun/Taheiho, 30th September, 1925.

Chinese version
(Duplicate)

[K.—19]

AIGUN Despatch No. 239 to I.G.

Appendix No.

為奉令查愛琿關所屬口岸機製洋式貨物暨機製麪粉等項運往外洋及通商口岸每年價值並該貨運單所貼印花稅價按年詳細查覆等因奉此謹將各項機製洋式貨物麪粉及印花稅價各項價值詳列於左

計開

一愛琿本口機製洋式貨物運往外洋每年價值查自民國三年至十三年此十一年間每年並無該項貨物價值

二愛琿本口機製洋式貨物運往通商口岸每年價值查自民國三年至十三年此十一年間每年並無該項貨物價值

三愛琿本口機製麪粉運往外洋及通商口岸每年價值查自民國三年至十年此八年間愛琿關為濱江關所屬一切統計由濱江關辦理於民國十一年一月一日起所有統計奉令自行出理民國十一年價值為關平銀六十八萬八千六百二十五兩十二年關平銀二十九萬八千七百八十九兩十三年關平銀十五萬五百五十五兩

[K.—21]

四厦门关所发机制洋式货物机制麸粉运单贴用印花税价查自民国三

年至十三年每年并每收此项印花价值

所有奉令查明各项价值谨呈

总税务司查核

厦门关税务司贺智兰谨呈

中华民国十年　九月　三十日

呈海关总税务司署 239 号文　　　　瑷珲关 1925 年 9 月 30 日

尊敬的海关总税务司（北京）：

根据海关总税务司署第 3641 号令：

“统计报告：税务处要求汇报 1914 年至 1924 年机制洋式货物出口价值、机制面粉出口价值报告及货运单所贴印花税价报告。”

兹呈送各项报告。

您忠诚的仆人

贺智兰（R. F. C. Hedgeland）

瑷珲关税务司

瑷珲关致海关总税务司署第 239 号呈附件

（1）1914 年至 1924 年 11 年间，瑷珲关运往外洋之机制洋式货物价值：

查无该项货物价值

（2）1914 年至 1924 年 11 年间，瑷珲关运往通商口岸之机制洋式货物价值：

查无该项货物价值

（3）1914 年至 1924 年 11 年间，瑷珲关运往外洋及通商口岸之机制面粉价值：

1914—1921 年：无数据。虽然瑷珲关已于 1921 年 10 月 1 日起从哈尔滨关独立出来，但直至 1921 年末，瑷珲关的一切统计仍由哈尔滨关办理。自 1922 年 1 月 1 日起，瑷珲关所有统计奉令自行办理（参阅海关总税务司署第 1/85630 号令）。

1922 年：688625 海关两

1923 年：298789 海关两

1924 年：150555 海关两

（4）1914 年至 1924 年 11 年间，瑷珲关机制洋式货物和机制面粉出口运单粘贴印花税价：

查无此项印花税价

贺智兰（R. F. C. Hedgeland）

瑷珲关税务司

1925 年 9 月 30 日，瑷珲关 / 大黑河

16. 为指示未遵守满洲特别免重征执照管理规定者实施处罚办法事

INDEXED

334
I.G.

No. 334 COMMRS.

Aigun No. 111,481

INSPECTORATE GENERAL OF CUSTOMS,

PEKING, 3rd March 1927.

Sir,

I am directed by the Officiating Inspector General to append copy of correspondence with the Moukden Commissioner in connection with the refusal of the Tax Offices in Manchuria to recognise and stamp Manchurian Special Exemption Certificates issued after 15th January last, and to request you to follow the instructions of his despatch No. 782/111,475 to the Moukden Commissioner in regard to the enforcement of the penalties laid down in the regulations relative to the failure to return within four months from date of issue Manchurian Special Exemption Certificates, duly stamped in proof of arrival by the Tax Office at the mart of destination.

I am,

Sir,

Your obedient Servant,

R. Yoshimoto

Officiating Chief Secretary.

Appendix.

Commissioner of Customs,

AIGUN.

A P P E N D I X.

Copy of Moukden Despatch No. 749 to I. G.

No. 749 | Custom House,
I. G. | Moukden, 24th February 1927.

Sir,

In my despatch No. 745 I reported that the Fengtien Commissioner for Foreign Affairs had notified me that the issue of Special Manchurian Exemption Certificates was to cease from the 16th January, and that, pending receipt of instructions from yourself, I was continuing to issue such Certificates as might be applied for.

Since the 15th January the British-American Tobacco Company has been the only applicant for Special Manchurian Exemption Certificates, which are issued by this office in exchange for original Certificates issued at the port of importation (Circular No. 1730).

The B. A. T. Co. has now returned to me for cancellation a number of Certificates, issued since the 15th January, and notified me that, owing to the refusal of the Tax officials at marts of destination to recognise these documents, the Company is unable to comply with Rule 1 of the regulations governing the issue of Special Exemption Certificates, which requires that Certificates must be returned to the Commissioner of Customs who issued them within four months from date

of

of issue, duly stamped in proof of arrival by the Tax Office at the mart of destination. In one case reported to me by the Company the Tax Office has retained a Certificate and refuses to surrender it.

When returning these Certificates, the B. A. T. Co. asked me for a written assurance that it will not be held liable for the penalty laid down in Rule 2 of the regulations for failure to comply with Rule 1, seeing that the Tax Offices refuse to recognise or stamp any Certificate issued after the 15th January.

I have informed the Company that I am referring this request to you, and I have the honour to ask whether I may waive the penalties laid down in Rule 2 in view of the fact that holders of Special Manchurian Exemption Certificates issued since 15th January cannot, under present conditions, comply with the requirement of Rule 1 owing to the absolute refusal of the Tax Offices to recognise these documents .

I have etc.,

(Signed) R. L. Warren,

Commissioner.

Copy of I. G. Despatch No. 782 to Moukden.

No. 782. Commrs.
Moukden No.111,475.

Peking, 3rd March 1927.

Sir,

I am directed by the Officiating Inspector General to acknowledge receipt of your despatch No. 749 :

reporting that holders of Special Manchurian Exemption Certificates are unable to comply with the regulation requiring that Certificates must be returned within four months from date of issue duly stamped in proof of arrival by the Tax Office at the mart of destination owing to the refusal of the Tax Officials at marts of destination to recognise these documents; and enquiring whether in the circumstances you may waive the penalties laid down in the regulations :

and, in reply, to say that you may waive the penalties in regard to Certificates issued between the 16th January and the date of receipt of this despatch in consideration of the fact that the Company concerned may not have been aware that the Tax Offices would refuse to recognise and stamp Certificates issued after the former date. You are to inform the Company concerned accordingly, but are to add that the regulations will

be

be applied and the penalties enforced strictly in respect to Certificates issued after receipt of this despatch. Similar information is to be given to all other applicants for Special Manchurian Exemption Certificates, who should be given to understand that the Customs procedure in connection with the issue of these Certificates remains unaltered and that, if the local authorities refuse to stamp the Certificates, it is to their Consular Authorities that they should apply for redress.

I am, etc.,

(Signed) H. Kishimoto,

Officiating Chief Secretary.

True copies:

C. M. P...

Acting Assistant Secretary.

致瑷珲关第 334/111481 号令　　海关总税务司署（北京）1927 年 3 月 3 日

尊敬的瑷珲关税务司：

奉代理总税务司命令，兹附与奉天关税务司之间的通信，信件内容有关满洲税捐局拒绝承认自 1927 年 1 月 15 日起发放的满洲特别免重征执照，并拒绝在执照上贴印花税票，敬请贵方遵照代理总税务司致奉天关第 782/111745 号令指示，未能在满洲特别免重征执照发放期间（货物目的地的税捐局正式盖章证明到货）四个月内返还者，需根据条例规定实施处罚。

您忠诚的仆人

岸本广吉（H. Kishimoto）

代理总务科税务司

附件

奉天关致海关总税务司署第749号呈副本

呈海关总税务司公第749号文　　　　奉天关1927年2月24日

奉天关第745号呈报告了奉天交涉员署已通知奉天关,自1月16日起停止发放满洲特别免重征执照,等待海关总税务司署进一步指令,如可以申请,则继续发放此执照。

自1月15日起,只有英美烟草公司申请了满洲特别免重征执照,由奉天关发放以换取进口的口岸颁布的原始执照(第1730号通令)。

英美烟草公司现已将1月15日起发放的大量执照退回并作废,并告知奉天关,由于驻货物目的地的税捐局拒绝承认这些执照,其公司无法遵守满洲里特别免重征执照(颁发管理条例第一条,其中规定满洲里特别免重征执照必须于发放后四个月内返还至颁发的海关税务司,由驻货物目的地的税捐局盖章证明到货。英美烟草公司向奉天关报告,税捐局已扣留一份执照并且拒绝交出此执照。

在退还其余执照时,英美烟草公司要求奉天关出具一份书面保证,鉴于税捐局拒绝承认自1月15日起发放的执照,其不会因未能遵守条例第一条而受到条例第二条规定的处罚。

奉天关已通知英美烟草公司,该关已向海关总税务司署提交此申请,鉴于税捐局无条件拒绝承认自1月15日发放的满洲特别免重征执照,英美烟草公司当前情况下绝无可能遵守条例第一条规定,申请免除处罚。

您忠诚的仆人

霍李家(R.L.Warren)

奉天关税务司

海关总税务司署致奉天关第782号令副本

致奉天关第782/111475号令　　　　海关总税务司署（北京）1927年3月3日

第749号呈收悉：

"条例规定满洲特别免重征执照（目的地税捐局正式盖章证明到货）必须于发放后四个月内返还，但是由于目的地税捐局拒绝承认这些执照，执照持有人无法遵守此条例；询问此情况下能否免除条例中处罚。"

奉代理总税务司命令，现批复如下：兹告知，鉴于英美烟草公司未能得知税捐局会拒绝承认1月16日后发放的执照，凡持有1月16日起至此令接收日之间发放的执照者，奉天关可免除对其的处罚。奉天关须将豁免事宜告知英美烟草公司，此外须告知其此令接收日期之后发放的执照，将会严格执行条例规定及处罚。奉天关须将此指令告知其他满洲特别免重征执照申请人，使其理解发放此执照的海关规程不变，如税捐局拒绝盖章，则申请人须向其领事机构申请补偿。

您忠诚的仆人

岸本广吉（H. Kishimoto）

代理总务科税务司

此副本内容真实有效，特此证明。确认人签字：裴德生（C. M. Potterson）

代理总务科副税务司

17. 为瑷珲关将检查中外人等护照事宜全权移交地方警察接办事

FOREIGN PASSPORTS: EXAMINATION AND CONTROL OF: Copy of Taoyin's despatch reporting the receipt of Civil Governor's instructions that entire charge of , be taken by police, forwarding: instructions in re requesting.

342. 342 I.G.

I.G.

Aigun, 23rd November, 1927.

Sir,

I have the honour to refer to you for your consideration and instructions copy of a despatch received from the Taoyin on the 18th instant informing me of the receipt of instructions from the Civil Governor that the examination and control of passports of foreigners should be entirely in the hands of the police.

Copy appended

In quoting as a precedent the change in procedure in this connection at the Kirin ports of the Harbin district, it was not plain in my mind as to whether the new regulations were to apply to foreigners crossing the frontier at Taheiho and Aigun. On consulting the Taoyin on this point he told me that they were to apply to all foreigners whether arriving by

The Inspector General of Customs,

Peking.

by steamer from river ports or crossing the frontier. As to Chinese, who only carry passports when crossing the frontier, he stated that he had no instructions as to any change of practice with respect to them and we could suit ourselves as to whether or not we continued to visè such passports.

The practice has been for some time that both the police and the Customs visèd all passports. This has meant an unnecessary duplication of work and it would seem to me well if the visèing of such documents, whether Chinese or foreign, were left entirely to the police in the future. Their passport bureau is now fairly well organised and can carry on.

The Customs passport procedure now in force was introduced in 1920 by orders of the Harbin Commissioner, before this port was separated from Harbin, and no Inspectorate correspondence regarding the subject is on file

in

in this office.

I have the honour to be,

Sir,

Your obedient Servant,

[signature]

Acting Commissioner.

Appendix.

Chinese version sent to I.G. in Aigun despatch no. 344.

FOREIGN PASSPORTS: EXAMINATION AND CONTROL OF: Chinese version, in duplicate, of Aigun despatch No.342 to I.G. in re, as called for by Chinese Secretary, forwarding. 344 I.G.

344. Registered.

I.G. Aigun 16th December, 1927.

Sir,

In accordance with the instructions of Chinese Secretary's Memo. of 3rd December, 1927:

directing me to forward a Chinese version, in duplicate, of Aigun despatch No. 342 to I. G., regarding the relinquishment of Passport Control:

I have the honour to forward, herewith, two copies of a Chinese version of the above mentioned despatch, one appended and the other enclosed.

I have the honour to be,

Sir,

Your obedient Servant,

[signature]

Acting Commissioner.

Appendix.

The Inspector General of Customs,

Peking.

呈

第三百四十二號

呈為具報檢查外人護照改歸警察接辦等情仰祈
鑒核示遵事案竊於民國十六年十一月十八日准黑河道尹兼璦琿
交涉員第六百十一號來函内開案查前奉省令以松黑兩江停輪
碼頭檢查外人護照事宜向由地方警察會同海關辦理現在松
花江沿江海關檢查外人護照事項業由警察接辦所有黑龍江

沿江海關檢查外人護照事宜亦應歸由警察接辦並令仿照吉省
規章規定檢查所章程及檢查規則各一份呈明公布施行等因當
經叅照吉省規章擬具黑龍江沿江各口岸檢查外國人出入境護照
規則及檢查所章程各一份呈請核示去後茲奉省長第一零九三三
號指令内開呈件均悉查所擬檢查所章程及檢查規則大致均屬

妥協應准照辦仰即分別公布尅日飭警接辦並將接收開辦日期具報等因奉此除分令接辦及公布外相應函請貴稅務司查照飭屬交代並布見復為荷等因到關查吉林所屬之哈爾濱區域內各商埠對於檢查外人護照事宜現已變更新章此可援為先例惟未審該新章應否施行於黑愛二埠出入邊界之外人關於此項問題曾向

黑河道尹徵求意見據云該新章僅祇對於外人由沿江口岸乘船來
往或出入邊界者一律施行至於華人攜帶護照出入邊界其檢查
手續應否變更現尚未有明令海關可以自行酌奪辦理等語查
檢查護照事宜向由海關與地方警察雙方會同辦理此項辦法含
有重複之意實則無須海關檢查蓋因黑河警察廳所設之驗照處

頗稱完善以署稅務司之意無論中外人等護照其檢查事宜似可
完全移歸地方警察接辦以專責成惟查本關辦理檢查護照事宜
始於民國九年彼時本關爲濱江關分關係奉該關稅務司令施行
關於此項問題與
總署一切來往文件本關無案可稽所有檢查各項護照事宜擬請

完全移歸地方警察辦理各緣由是否有當理合具文呈請

鑒核示遵施行謹呈

代理總稅務司

愛琿關署稅務司鐸博賚

Registered.

385
I.G.

385 COMMRS.

No. 115,686

INSPECTORATE GENERAL OF CUSTOMS,

PEKING, 14th January 1928.

Sir,

With reference to your despatches Nos. 342 and 344 :

Foreign Passports: examination and control of: copy of Taoyin's despatch reporting the receipt of Civil Governor's instructions that entire charge of to be taken by police, forwarding: instructions in re requesting:

I append, for your information and guidance, copy of Shui-wu Ch'u despatch No. 31, from which you will see that all work in connection with passport inspection, and control at Aigun is to be handed over to the Police Administration.

You are requested to act accordingly in consultation with the Taoyin, and to note that these instructions are to apply equally to all work in connection with the viséing of passports of Chinese.

When

Commissioner of Customs,

AIGUN.

When the Passport Service is finally handed over to the Police the fact should be reported by despatch, with Chinese version in duplicate, for the information of the Shui-wu Ch'u.

I am,

Sir,

Your obedient Servant,

Officiating Inspector General.

Appendix.

稅務處令第三一號中華民國十七年一月十二日

據代理總稅務司呈稱案查民國十五年十一月間曾奉令開濱江關檢查外人護照事宜應改歸警察接辦等因當經轉令該關稅務司遵照辦理旋於十六年十月間將該關遵令移交情形備文呈請鑒核在案茲據愛琿關署稅務司呈稱准黑河道尹並愛琿交涉員函稱奉省令松黑兩江停輪碼頭檢查外人護照事宜向由地方警察會同海關辦理現在松花江沿江海關檢查外人護照事項業由警察接辦所有黑龍江沿江海關檢查外人護照事宜亦應歸警察接辦等因應函請查照飭屬交代並希見復等因嗣又向黑河道尹徵求意見據云新章僅對於由沿江口岸乘船來往或出入邊界者一律施行至華人攜帶護照出入邊界其檢查手續應否變更現尚未有明令海關可自行酌奪辦理等語查檢查護照事宜向由海關與地方警察雙方會同辦理實則無須海關檢查蓋因黑河警察廳所設之驗照處頗稱完善以署稅務司之意無論中外人等護照其檢查事宜似可完全移歸地方警察接

辦以事責成是否有當理合呈請鑒核示遵等情查愛琿關在未成為獨立海關以前原屬濱江關分關其辦理驗查護照事宜係與濱江關同時舉辦現在黑龍江省長官既請將驗查外人護照事宜收歸警察接辦擬請即由鈞處核准飭行援照濱江關成案轉令愛琿關稅務司遵將檢查中外人護照事宜一律移交警察辦理再按該關稅務司原呈內載有警察廳所設之驗照處頗稱完善等語據代理總稅務司之意所有該關驗查護照事宜如蒙准予移交警察接辦似可飭令立即交代毋庸援照濱江關辦法先由警察會同執行稽查練習俟經過一定時期後再行移交接管理合備文呈請鑒核示復以憑轉飭該關稅務司遵照等情前來查濱江關驗查外人來華護照一案民國十五年十一月間曾由外交部會財政部分別咨商黑龍江省長與吉林省長後改歸地方警察辦理當經本處于是年第一〇〇五號令行知代理總稅務司轉令濱江關稅務司遵辦有案至原隸濱江關之愛琿分關因改為獨立海關尚未將檢查中外人護照事宜移交茲經黑河道尹兼愛琿交涉員

函請改歸警察接辦代理總稅務司擬請准令立即交代毋庸援照濱江關先行練習再行移交辦法自屬正辦應即照准除分行外交財政等部暨黑龍江省長查照外相應令行代理總稅務司轉令愛琿關稅務司遵照移交可也此令

文桂同校
周啓明

PASSPORT CONTROL: date of handing over to local Police, notifying. Chinese version of despatch in duplicate, forwarding.

353
I.G.

353.

I.G.

Aigun 7th February, 1928.

Sir,

With reference to I. G. despatch No. 385/115,686 to Aigun:

transmitting the instructions of the Shui-wu Ch'u that all control of Passports at Aigun, whether such documents are carried by Chinese or foreigners, is to be handed over to the local Police:

I have the honour to inform you that, on receipt of the above despatch, arrangements were duly made with the Heiho Taoyin to carry out the instructions contained therein. A copy of the Taoyin's letter fixing the date of the formal transfer of control to the Police as the 1st February, 1928, is appended.

Appendix No.1.

A Chinese version in duplicate, as instructed, is also forwarded, one appended and

Appendix No.2.

the

The Inspector General of Customs,

Peking.

the other enclosed, for the information of the Shui-wu Ch'u.

I have the honour to be,

Sir,

Your obedient Servant,

Acting Commissioner.

Appendix

Enclosure to Aigun No.353 to I. G.

呈第三百五十三號

呈為具報遵令將本關稽查中外人等護照事宜移交地方警察接

辦日期仰祈

鑒核備案事查本關稽查中外人等護照事宜移交地方警察接辦

一案曾於本年一月二十七日呈奉

總稅務司令轉奉

税務處第三一號令開所有本關稽查中外人等護照事宜准令立即交代等因奉此署税務司遵即擬將稽查中外人等護照事宜於本年二月一日完全移交地方警察接收除令愛琿分關遵照外並曾經備具道字第二二七號函達黑河道尹請其分别轉令地方警察机關務於二月一日接收去後旋准第四七號復函内開案准貴税務司道字第二二

中華民國十七年二月七日

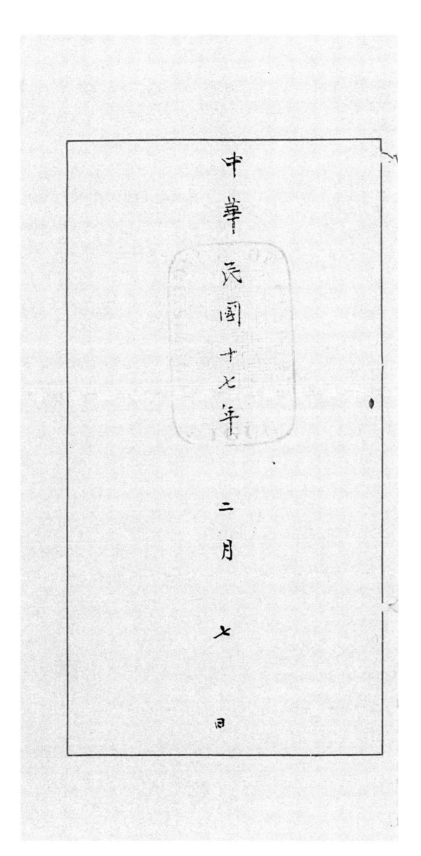

呈海关总税务司署 342 号文　　　　　　　　　　瑷珲关 1927 年 11 月 23 日

尊敬的海关总税务司（北京）：

道尹于 11 月 18 日致函瑷珲关，传达省长命令——由警察全权负责外人护照的检查和管理工作。本署现将此事呈报，请予以指示。

虽然哈尔滨关吉林口岸已有变更管理章程之先例，但本署并不确定新章程是否适用于通过大黑河与瑷珲边境入境的洋人，遂向道尹咨询此事。道尹回复，凡通过口岸或边境入境之洋人，均应遵循新章程。但对于只携带护照出境之华人，道尹则表示尚未收到任何要求更改惯例的指令，海关可自行决定是否要继续签注此类护照。

按照之前的惯例，签注护照一事必须由海关和警察共同执行，这无疑既浪费了时间又浪费了人力。且警察局护照办事处现组织有序，完全具备独立执行护照签注的能力，因此本署赞同今后由警察全权负责华人及外人的护照签注工作。

早在 1920 年，瑷珲关还未从哈尔滨关分离之时，就已经奉哈尔滨关税务司的命令，开始办理海关护照手续。不过海关总税务司署的相关信函，本署却并未存档。

您忠诚的仆人

铎博赉（R. M. Talbot）

瑷珲关署理税务司

此副本抄送至哈尔滨关税务司

录事：屠守鑫四等二级帮办

呈海关总税务司署 344 号文　　瑷珲关 1927 年 12 月 16 日

尊敬的海关总税务司（北京）：

根据 1927 年 12 月 3 日总务科税务司通函：

“请呈交瑷珲关致海关总税务司署第 342 号呈（有关放弃外人护照管理权一事）之中文版本，一式两份。”

兹附瑷珲关第 342 号呈的中文版抄件，一份附录，一份附件。

您忠诚的仆人

铎博赉（R. M. Talbot）

瑷珲关署理税务司

录事：屠守鑫　四等二级帮办

致瑷珲关第385/115686号令　　　　海关总税务司署（北京）1928年1月14日

尊敬的瑷珲关税务司：

根据第342号及第344号呈：

“外国护照：道尹函件称已收到省长指令，将外国护照查验事宜全权移交警察管理；请示相关指示。”

为了便于贵署顺利执行，兹附税务处第31号令，以供参考。据该令所示，瑷珲关有关护照的一切查验及管理工作移交至警察厅。

请向道尹咨询，按此令照办。贵署需注意，上述指令同等适用于华人，有关中国护照开具的一切工作也应交由警办。护照业务完全移交警察后，须发呈禀报，中文版，一式两份，供税务处参考。

您忠诚的仆人

易纨士（A. H. F. Edwardes）

代理海关总税务司

呈海关总税务司署 353 号文　　　　　　　　瑷珲关 1928 年 2 月 7 日

尊敬的海关总税务司（北京）：

根据海关总税务司署致瑷珲关第 385/115686 号令：

"转达税务处指令——瑷珲关将检查中外人等护照事宜全权移交地方警察接办。"

兹报告，本署收到指令后，便立即与黑河道尹商定指令实施办法，拟将检查中外人等护照事宜于 1928 年 2 月 1 日完全移交地方警察接办。兹附道尹信函中文版抄件。一式两份，一份附录，一份附件，供税务处参阅。

您忠诚的仆人

铎博赉（R. M. Talbot）

瑷珲关署理税务司

此副本抄送至滨江关税务司

录事：屠守鑫四等二级帮办

18. 为指示出口需要农工部畜牧产品卫生检验检疫局颁发的检验合格证事

406
I.G.

No. 406 COMMRS.　　　　INSPECTORATE GENERAL OF CUSTOMS,

Aigun No. 117,071.　　　　PEKING, 16th May 1928.

Sir,

1. I append, for your information and guidance, copies of Shui-wu Ch'u despatches Nos. 147 and 312, from which you will see that the Ministry of Agriculture and Labour having drawn up detailed regulations to cover the inspection of Wools, Hides, Meats, etc., for export abroad, the Ch'u instructs that in future meat and animal casings are only to be allowed to be exported abroad if accompanied by an Inspection Certificate issued by the Bureau of Veterinary and Sanitary Inspection of Animal Products of the Ministry of Agriculture and Labour, a <u>pro forma</u> of which is enclosed, and that if any difficulties arise in connection with this procedure, full details thereof are to be reported to the Ch'u for transmission to the Ministry of Agriculture and Labour for settlement.

2. In the event of a Bureau of Veterinary and Sanitary Inspection of Animal Products of the Ministry of Agriculture and Labour being established at your port, therefore, I have to request that you will consult with the Superintendent and issue a joint notification to the public to the effect that, in accordance with Article 5 of the Detailed Regulations governing the Operation of the Ministry of Agriculture and

The Commissioner of Customs,

A I G U N.

and Labour Regulations for the inspection of Wools, Hides, Meats, etc., for export abroad, the export abroad of meat and animal casings will only be permitted by the Customs in future on production of an Inspection Certificate obtainable from the Bureau of Veterinary and Sanitary Inspection of Animal Products.

3. You are to note, however, that the Inspection Certificates are only to be required for meat and animal casings and not for the other articles detailed in the Regulations, and, moreover, that the new procedure is not to be put into force until a joint notification, signed by the Superintendent and yourself has been duly issued.

4. If, after the new regulations are put into force, difficulties arise owing to their enforcement, a report giving full details thereof is to be submitted, with Chinese version in duplicate, for transmission to the Shui-wu Ch'u.

5. Finally, no change is to be made in your present practice in regard to the export of meat and animal casings abroad pending the establishment at your port of the aforesaid Bureau, and when and if such establishment takes place and the new regulations are duly enforced, the fact is to be reported to me for purposes of record.

I am,

Sir,

Your obedient Servant,

Officiating Inspector General.

稅務處令第一四七號　中華民國十七年二月二十八日

案准農工部咨開案查美國禁銷中國肉類一事以我國無正式檢查機關及畜牧衛生行政長官或專門獸疫人員簽字執照所有中國肉類禁止運美銷售等因嗣經京外肉商呈請速設是項檢查機關以圖救濟本部爲挽救海外商業並爲維持國際貿易信用起見擬定檢查條例彙經呈請

大元帥公布並訂定組織章程及施行細則在案除飭將該所在津剋期成立依法辦理檢查及簽發護照外所有以前各種運銷護照處行取銷嗣後非有該所正式簽字執照一律禁運出口應請轉知各海關一體遵照並請轉令該關臨時彙令各商先行赴所領照方准報關出口藉資取締准此次該所辦理檢查事宜係先就腸衣肉類兩項填發執照至毛革兩項一俟籌備就緒再行咨達一體辦理等因當經本處以美國禁止我國肉製食品運美銷售一案民國十二年七月間內務部曾經擬定出口肉類檢驗條例呈准公布咨照本處通令各關遵辦並將部派各關檢驗員隨時知照本處令關接洽有案此次

農工部所送之毛革肉類出口檢查條例其中辦法頗有出入究竟此項兩種規定不同之條例應如何辦理似應由農工部邀與內務部接洽妥當後咨明本處爰抄錄內務部前咨及出口肉類檢查條例各一分咨送農工部查照辦理在案旋准農工部復稱查本案於民國十六年十月十二日由國務會議議決此案應歸農工部主管並責成農工部迅籌根本辦法以重畜產而維商業等因嗣於同月十九日由本部提交國務會議擬就通商口岸先行設立毛革肉類檢查所實行檢查出口物品以維對外信用並制定條例九條提議議決以便施行當於同月二十五日准國務院函開准農工部提出擬就通商口岸設立毛革肉類檢查所訂定出口檢查條例九條請議決施行一案茲經國務會議議決照辦由農工部呈請指令公布等因應函達查照辦理嗣於十一月五日奉

大元帥指令呈悉准如所擬辦理此令等因奉此是本案應歸本部主管已無容疑除將檢查條例及執照式樣咨送外交部並轉達駐京美使外茲將檢查條例及簽字執照式樣咨送貴處即希查照前咨分令各關一體遵辦並准內務部咨稱查此案業經農工部

呈奉

大元帥令准應請分令各關遵辦各等因前來本處查原訂之出口肉類檢查條例前准內務部來咨曾經本處於民國十二年第九五零號令行知代理總稅務司轉令各關稅務司遵辦在案茲既准農工內務等部咨稱前因自應改照新章辦理相應檢同農工部新訂之毛革肉類出口檢查條例並施行細則及執照式樣各三十份令行代理總稅務司轉令各關稅務司遵照新頒條例辦理並曉諭各商先行赴所領照方准報運出口以資取締此令

稅務處令第三一一二號 中華民國十七年四月十二日

准農工部咨開頃據毛革肉類出口檢查所呈稱案查津海關稅務司對於職所腸衣出口執照發生問題一案經局主任羅龐由京返津後即赴稅務司與之接洽據稱已奉有北京總稅務司來函謂關於職所檢查執照已承認有效並准取消何克簽字但令津海關不得強迫衆商非持職所執照方准出口云云據該稅務司之解釋即對於職所執照

臨承認有效而商人憑織所執照者亦准出口之語似此承認而非承認之表示核與織所施行細則第五條之規定已相牴觸將來腸衣運往美國者固可來織所領照而運銷他處者盡可無須領照若不及早解決一聽海關任意放行實於檢查前途有礙為此呈請鈞部咨請稅務處轉飭總稅務司仍行電令津埠稅務司對於織所執照依織所施行細則第五條規定辦理以利進行等情查此案迭經本部咨請稅務處轉令總稅務司辦理在案茲據該所所稱各節是該稅務司仍未完全遵照辦理長此以往運出之肉類既不能一律檢驗難保不再發生拒絕征運情事國信華商俱蒙影響為此咨請查照原案再行令知總稅務司轉令各關稅務司對於肉商之報關徵稅無論運往何處既須遵照檢查條例施行細則第五條辦理並希將辦理情形見復等因前來本處查農工部所訂肉類出口檢查條例及施行細則無非為便利肉類運銷國外起見所有該細則第五條之規定在海關自可執行依照辦理即或因此發生若何問題亦可隨時報由本處轉商農工部設法解決除函復農工部外相應令行代理總稅務司轉令津海關稅務司遵照可也此令

文桂

明同校

致瑷珲关第406/117071号令　　　　海关总税务司署（北京）1928年5月16日

尊敬的瑷珲关税务司：

1. 为了便于贵署顺利执行，兹附税务处第147号和第312号令，以供参考。据该令所示，农工部已制定详细规定，规范毛、革、肉类等出口检查；税务处命令，今后肉类及肠衣出口时，必须有农工部畜牧产品卫生检验检疫局签发的检验合格证，随函附上检验合格证模板；检验合格证办理过程中如有任何困难，请将问题详情汇报至税务处，转呈农工部解决。

2. 如果农工部畜牧产品卫生检验检疫局正在贵口岸设立，请贵署咨询海关监督，向公众发布联合通知，大意是根据《农工部毛革肉类出口检查条例施行细则》第5条，今后肉类及肠衣如经海关批准出口，必须领有畜牧产品卫生检验检疫局签发的检验合格证。

3. 但是，贵署须注意，只有肉类及肠衣须办理检验合格证，细则中的其他物品无须办理此合格证。此外，只有经海关监督和贵署签发联合通知，方可施行此办法。

4. 新细则施行后，如果由此引发问题，须就此问题详细呈上报告，报告需用中文，一式两份，转呈税务处。

5. 畜牧产品卫生检验检疫局在贵口岸完成设立前，贵口岸仍按惯例处理肉类与肠衣出口，无须更改。畜牧产品卫生检验检疫局设立时，新细则正式生效，届时请写呈上报，以便归档。

您忠诚的仆人

易纨士（A. H. F. Edwardes）

代理海关总税务司

19. 为传达关务署有关由瑷珲关出口土产皮货的征税办法规定事

A.—19

4159
I.G.

SHANGHAI OFFICE OF THE
INSPECTORATE GENERAL OF CUSTOMS,
SHANGHAI,
~~PEKING,~~ 22nd May, 1929.

No. 459 COMMRS.

Aigun No. 121,590

Registered.

Sir,

I append, for your information and guidance, copy of Kuan-wu Shu despatch No. 598, from which you will see that a complaint has been received from skin dealers at Hei-ho that skins of animals caught in China have to pay the same duty at Aigun as foreign imported skins, and claiming that they should only pay export duty at 5% ad valorem on being exported abroad; and that the Shu requires a detailed report as to whether skins which are exported from Aigun are charged import duty or whether special circumstances exist which require special treatment.

I have to request you to prepare a report on the matter giving as full particulars as possible and to submit it under cover of a despatch with Chinese version in duplicate.

I am,
Sir,
Your obedient Servant,

Inspector General.

Appendix.

The Commissioner of Customs,
A I G U N.

財政部關務署訓令第五九八號 中華民國十八年五月十五日

令總稅務司梅樂和

爲令行事准東北政務委員會咨開案據黑龍江省政府主席萬福麟呈稱據黑河市政籌備處電據黑河北記洋行呈稱查自二月一日起按照新訂稅則海關對於入口貨物凡貨物自國外收到者係按百分之二二五征收此地瑷琿江關對於國外皮貨與本地中國獵人在中國境內獲得之皮貨混爲一談殊不知本地皮貨如發往倫敦應照皮貨出口價值百分之五征收敝號購貨地點均在中國境內由中國棲林獵人手中購買外國皮貨毫未收購此事可由中國商人及黑河商會證明請訓令瑷琿江關對於敝號向倫敦發寄皮貨時照中國當地出產之皮貨按出口貨值百抽五征稅實爲德便等情據此查洋商每屆冬令來黑收買皮張除白狐外大都均係本省出產此項當地所收皮張運發外國當然應按出口稅率收稅惟瑷琿關稅務司向照國外皮貨進口稅率收稅從前進口稅輕洋商尚無異言今新稅則業已實行如仍前按進

口稅率征稅雖免洋商因稅重停止收買查黑河沿邊一帶出產大宗皮張如果洋商因此停收影響邊地皮業殊非淺鮮應請咨商財政部轉飭該關稅務司准照出口稅率收稅以維邊地皮業等情據此除指令候咨請核示再行飭遵外咨部查核見復以憑飭遵等因查黑河所出皮張既屬國產如經商人報運出口自不應適用進口稅率征收出口稅項現在璦琿關對於前項皮張出口是否係按進口新稅則征稅有無誤征情事抑有特殊情形應予分別征稅仰該總稅務司迅即轉飭查明呈復以憑核辦

此令

文郁
劉連勛 同校

Kuan-wu Shu despatch No.598 to I. G.

A despatch has been received from the North-Eastern Executive Council stating that according to a despatch from General Wan Fu-lin, Chairman of the Heilungkiang Province, it is stated that a telegram was received from the Heiho Provisional Mayor which states that

a petition was received from the Wool & Fur Trading Co. Taheiho, stating that since the New Import Tariff was introduced from 1st February, foreign imported goods have to pay duty at 22½%, and the Aigun Customs has always been treating skins caught in China in the same way as those imported from abroad. Now as native skins should only pay export duty at 5% ad valorem, as the said company purchase their goods only from native hunters within Chinese territory, and as no skin was bought from foreign countries,——the latter fact can be attested by the Heiho Chamber of Commerce—— so the Aigun Customs might be instructed to levy an export duty at 5% ad valorem on their skins when sent to London.

[Mayor's] Provisional [Mayor's] Comments

Generally speaking, foreign merchants come to Taheiho in winter to purchase skins, most of which, with the exception of white fox, are products of this province. Such skins when exported abroad should undoubtedly pay export duty. Whereas the Aigun Customs has hitherto charged import duty, no complaints were made by foreign merchants before, as the rate of import duty was small. If the import duty is still charged after the introduction of the New Tariff, the foreign merchants would probably suspend their business, and it will seriously affect the skin industry along the frontier region. In order to foster the skin industry in the frontier, the Board of Finance might be requested to instruct the Aigun Commissioner to charge export duty.

[Kuan-wu Shu's] [words]

In view of the above, it is concluded that the skins exported from Taheiho are certainly native goods, and if exported abroad the import Tariff is not applicable to them. Now whether they are wrongly charged import duty by the Aigun Customs, or whether special circumstances exist which require special treatment, you are directed to instruct the Aigun Commissioner to see into the matter and to forward a detailed report for consideration.

428. DUTY TREATMENT: SKINS EXPORTED FROM AIGUN: query in re by Kuan-wu Shu; report on, with Chinese version in duplicate, as called for by Inspector General, submitting.

I. G. Registered. Aigun 17th June, 1929.

Sir,

I have the honour to acknowledge the receipt of your despatch No. 459/121,590 :

forwarding a copy of Kuan-wu Shu despatch No.598 to the effect that a complaint had been received from fur dealers at Aigun of Customs treatment accorded and calling for a report ;

and, in reply, to inform you that the practice of passing all furs as foreign imports when shipped from Aigun originated many years ago when there was little or no trapping on the Chinese side of the Amur and practically all furs passing through this port were smuggled across the frontier from Siberia at remote places.

With the closing of the Sino-Soviet frontier in 1923 by the Soviet Authorities and their establishment of a Government Fur Monopoly it can be said that the smuggling of furs from Siberia practically ceased. At the same time there came a greatly increased demand for furs from abroad leading to the opening of foreign fur

THE INSPECTOR GENERAL OF CUSTOMS,

S H A N G H A I.

fur buying agencies in Aigun. These agencies were prepared to buy skins in large quantities and offered prices for the various sorts that interested Chinese along the Amur and developed a native trapping industry.

The practice of treating furs as goods of foreign (Siberian) origin that had not paid duty was continued, however, as no protest was made, as some of the furs still came from Siberia and as many kinds would still pay the same duty of 5% whether classified as imports or exports.

With the introduction of the new Import Tariff on the 1st February, 1929, the tariff on furs was increased to 22½%, while during the winter preceding a great slump had occurred in the demand from abroad. This combination of high duties and lessened demand was acutely felt by dealers who appealed for a change of local practice and that all furs be classed henceforth as of native origin. I interviewed the Superintendent about the matter telling him the history of the present practice of treatment of furs and the complaints by dealers that were being made. He told me that he would refer the question to the Provincial Authorities which was done.

I have gone over the returns of furs passing through the Aigun Customs for the past few years and after careful inquiry as to their origin

origin I would classify them as follows:

Native.	Foreign.
Badger	Bear
Cat	Ermine
Dog	Fox, white
Deer	Lynk
Fox, grey	Otter
Fox, red	Sable
Goat	
Hare (rabbit)	
Marmot	
Raccoon	
Skunk	
Squirrel	
Weasel	
Wolf	

Of the furs listed as foreign very few appear in the local market at present so it may be said that practically all the furs dealt with now are of native origin. Should the frontier be reopened and the fur monopoly be abolished in Siberia, a contingency that seems remote, it is possible that smuggled furs might again make their appearance.

A Chinese version of this despatch is sent in duplicate, one appended and one enclosed.

I have the honour to be,

Sir,

Your obedient Servant,

[signature]

Acting Commissioner.

Appendix.

475
I.G.

[4.—29]

Registered. SHANGHAI OFFICE OF THE

No. 475 COMMRS. INSPECTORATE GENERAL OF CUSTOMS,

Aigun No. 122,713 Shanghai, ~~PEKING~~, 23rd July, 1929.

Sir,

With reference to your despatch No. 428:

forwarding, in reply to I.G. despatch No. 459/121,590, a report on your office practice of passing all furs as foreign imports when shipped from Aigun;

I append, for your information and guidance, copy of Kuan-wu Shu despatch No. 892, from which you will see that the Shu rules that this practice is to be discontinued, and that native skins on exportation are to pay duty according to the Export Tariff; but that as Aigun is on the Sino-Russian frontier care must be taken to see that skins which are not of native origin pay duty according to the Import Tariff.

You are requested to act accordingly.

I am,

Sir,

Your obedient Servant,

(Signed)

For Inspector General.

Appendix.

Commissioner of Customs,

A I G U N.

財政部關務署指令第八九二號　中華民國十八年七月十六日

令總稅務司梅樂和

呈一件為查明由愛琿關出口皮張征稅情形復請鑒核由

呈悉查土貨出口應按出口稅則征收稅項現在新訂進口稅則對於皮貨既已增加稅率至值百抽二二五尤未便仍按慣例征收所有國產皮貨報運出口應即一律按照出口稅則征收以維邊地皮業惟愛琿地處邊陲毗連俄境此後該關對於非國產之皮貨仍應切實查驗按照進口稅則征收以符征稅核實之旨除由部咨復東北政務委員會外仰即轉飭遵照辦理為要此令

文　郁

李守理　同仪

致瑷珲关第 459/121590 号令　　海关总税务司署（上海）1929 年 5 月 22 日

尊敬的瑷珲关税务司：

为了便于贵署顺利执行，兹附关务署第 598 号令副本，以供参考。据该令所示，按照黑河皮货商人投诉称，在瑷珲关进行土产皮货出口时上缴的税款与国外进口皮货进口税一样高；黑河皮货商人认为在出口土产皮货时只需缴纳皮货价值 5% 的出口税；关务署要求瑷珲关详细报告该关对出口的皮货是否征收进口税，或是存在什么特殊情况，需要另行征税。

请瑷珲关就此事呈交报告，报告内容尽可能详尽完整，使用中文编写，一式两份，以呈文形式回复。

您忠诚的仆人

梅乐和（F. W. Maze）

海关总税务司

关务署致海关总税务司署第598号令

东北政务委员会令称，据黑龙江省政府主席万福麟将军呈，其已收到黑河市政筹备处电报，内容如下：

据黑河北记洋行请愿书称，自2月1日起推行新订进口税则以来，凡国外进口货物，一律按22.5%征税，而瑷珲关一直将国外进口皮货与中国本地猎人在中国境内获得的皮货混为一谈。现在凡土产皮货出口，应按照皮货出口价值5%征税。北记洋行在中国境内向中国猎人购买皮货，从未自国外购买皮货，此事可由黑河商会证明。故，可命令瑷珲关对北记洋行发往伦敦的皮货，按照出口皮货价值5%征收出口税。

一般而言，外商冬季来大黑河购买的皮货，除白狐外，大都为本省出产。此类皮货出口国外时当然应征税出口税。而到目前为止，瑷珲关一直按照国外皮货进口税率征税，先前进口税低，外商尚无不满。现今新订税则业已施行，如仍按进口税率征税，外商难免会因征税过重停止收货，严重影响黑河沿边一带皮货产业，或许可以请求财政部转令请瑷珲关税务司征收出口税。

由上述内容可知，由大黑河出口的皮货必定为国产，若出口国外，则不应征收进口税。目前瑷珲关是对该公司出口皮货误征了进口税，还是存有特殊情形需另行征税，请转令瑷珲关税务司，立即查明情况，并呈交详细报告。

呈海关总税务司署428号文　　　　瑷珲关1929年6月17日

尊敬的海关总税务司（上海）：

海关总税务司署第19/121590号令收悉：

“传达关务署第598号令副本，大意为瑷珲关皮货商人投诉其征税办法，关务署现要求瑷珲关呈送一份报告。”

现汇报如下：凡由瑷珲关运出的过往皮货均视为外国进口商品，这一惯例由来已久。当时黑龙江华岸沿线鲜有毛皮，几乎所有通过此口岸的皮货都是从偏远的西伯利亚边境走私来的。

随着1923年苏维埃政府关闭中俄边境，建立政府皮货垄断，西伯利亚的皮货走私才真正终止。同时，对国外进口皮货日益增长的需求促使国外毛皮采购代理商在瑷珲关开店营业。这些代理商预先购入大量的毛皮，在黑龙江沿线售卖各种华人喜欢的毛皮，发展起了本地毛皮产业。

将皮货视为未完税的原产地为国外（西伯利亚）的商品的惯例一直延续着。这些来自西伯利亚的皮货无论被分类成进口商品还是出口商品都征以5%的关税，一直未有反对意见。

尽管之前冬季进口需求大跌，但随着1929年2月1日新进口税则的颁发，皮货进口税率上涨到22.5%。高税收、低需求使得商人们请求改革当地惯例，将所有皮货归为土产货物。本署会见了海关监督，询问了此事，告知其皮货征税现行惯例的历史，以及商人投诉一事。海关监督告知本署，其会向省政府报告此事。

本署已查看了近几年瑷珲关过关皮货报表，经过对土货产地仔细询查，本署作以下分类：

土货	洋货
獾皮	熊皮
猫皮	貂皮
狗皮	狐狸皮（白色）
鹿皮	山猫皮
狐狸皮（灰色）	水獭皮
狐狸皮（红色）	黑貂皮

土货	洋货
山羊皮	
兔皮	
土拨鼠皮	
浣熊皮	
臭鼬皮	
松鼠皮	
鼬鼠皮	
狼皮	

鉴于列表上的产自国外的皮货现很少出现在当地市场上,因此可以说实际上交易的皮货都是土产货物。如果边境重开,废除西伯利亚皮毛垄断的可能性微乎其微,一旦放开垄断,走私皮货可能再次出现。

此信函的中文版已呈交,一式两份,一份附录,一份附件。

您忠诚的仆人

铎博赉(R. M. Talbot)

瑷珲关署理税务司

录事:黎彭寿　四等一级帮办

致瑷珲关第475/122713号令　　　　海关总税务司署(上海)1929年7月23日

尊敬的瑷珲关税务司:

根据第428号呈:

"为回复海关总税务司署第459/121590号令,汇报由瑷珲关进口国外皮货的征税情形。"

为了便于贵署顺利执行,兹附关务署第892号令副本,以供参考。据该令所示,关务署命令瑷珲关停止该征税办法,并要求国产出口皮货按照出口税则征税,又因瑷珲关地处中俄边境交界地区,需注意非国产皮货须按进口税则征税。

敬请遵照此令执行。

您忠诚的仆人

华善(P. R. Walsham)

受总税务司委托签发此文

20. 为汇报地方政府为改善消防将向由轮船及民船所运进口各货抽收经费事

LOCAL TAXATION: imports by steamer and junk to be taxed by local authorities for maintenance of an improved fire brigade: report on, submitting

559 559/I.G.

I.G.

AIGUN 27th May, 1931.

INDEXED

Sir,

1. I have the honour to forward, appended hereto, with English translation attached, copy of a notification issued by the Taheiho Provisional Mayor from which it will be seen that, commencing from the present navigation season, all imports by steamer and junk are to be taxed to provide additional funds for the maintenance of an improved fire brigade. The tax, which corresponds in all respects except in name to wharfage dues, has been divided into two categories, 1.- a charge of one dollar cent per pood on ordinary goods, and 2.- a charge of half a dollar cent per pood on daily necessities (rice, flour, oils and salt), and it is to be collected through the Harbin Shipping Syndicate for steamer-borne cargo, and through the Junk Guild for junk-borne goods. No encroachment on Customs control has been, or is likely to be, encountered, but, in view of the instructions of the Ministry of Finance regarding the abolition of Likin and of all other taxation of a similar nature, I consider it necessary to report the enforcement of these additional charges on cargo arriving at this port. As far as I have been able to ascertain, the imposition of these fees has been decided on locally without reference to, or special authority from, the Heilungkiang Provincial Government.

2. A Chinese version, in duplicate, of this report is forwarded, enclosed herewith.

I have the honour to be, Sir,

Your obedient Servant,

(Signed) C. H. B. Joly

(C. H. B. Joly)
Acting Commissioner.

The Inspector General of Customs,

S H A N G H A I.

Appendix No.1

Appendix No.1

(Translation)

HEIHO PROVISIONAL MAYOR'S NOTIFICATION

No. 1005.

The public is hereby notified that, in accordance with Resolution No. 2 passed by the 2nd Meeting of the Heiho Fire Prevention and Sanitation Committee, a fee for the maintenance of the Fire Brigade will be levied on all imports at the rate of one cent per pood for ordinary cargo, and half cent per pood for daily necessities (rice, flour, oils, and salt). The fee on all steamer-borne cargo will be collected by the Heiho Office of the Harbin Shipping Syndicate, and that on all junk-borne cargo by the Junk Guild, on behalf of the Committee.

Ch'i Chao-yü,
Provisional Mayor.

15th May, 20th year of the Chinese Republic.

True translation:
[signature]
4th Assistant A.

Appendix No.2.

[K.—21]

AIGUN DESPATCH NO. 559/I.G.

APPENDIX NO. 2.

黑河市政籌備處佈告第一〇〇五號

為佈告事案查本市消防衛生委員會第二次會議第二案議決為辦理消防起見擬進口貨物雜貨每布特抽收經費一分米面油鹽每布特抽收半分所有輪運各貨託由駐黑東北航務局代收風船所運各貨責成風船公會代收案關辦理地方公益函應認真辦理除分函令外合亟佈告商民人等一體遵照毋違此佈

處長齊肇豫

中華民國二十年五月十五日

True copy:

Actg. Commr.

20,000 / 11.28.

呈海关总税务司署559号文　　　　　　　　　　　　瑷珲关1931年5月27日

尊敬的海关总税务司(上海):

1. 兹附暂代黑河市政筹备处处长所发布告之抄件及其英文译本。从中可知,自今年航运季开始,地方政府将向轮船和民船所运进口各货抽收经费,以资改善消防。

此项收税除名称外均与码头捐一致,主要分为两类,普通货物每普特抽收一分,米面油盐等日常必需品每普特抽收半分,轮船所运各货将由东北航务局(即哈尔滨官商航业总联合局)代收,民船所运各货将由民船公会代收。

此项收税于海关管理上固无抵触情形,似乎亦不会有此可能,唯各项杂税厘捐,财政部曾有严令永远废除,故此将本埠开始抽收货物消防经费各缘由具文呈报。据查,此项收税乃由地方政府自行决定,并未提请黑龙江省政府批准。

2. 兹附此呈汉文译本,一式两份。

您忠诚的仆人

周骊(C. H. B. Joly)

瑷珲关署理税务司

附件 1

(译本)

黑河市政筹备处布告第 1005 号

为布告事：案查本市消防卫生委员会第二次会议第二案议决，为办理消防起见，于进口货物，杂货每普特抽收经费一分，米面油盐等每普特抽收半分，所有轮运各货，托由驻黑东北航务局代收，民船所运各货，责成民船公会代收。

齐肇豫

黑河市政筹备处处长

1931 年 5 月 15 日

此译本内容真实有效，特此证明：

录事：陈培因　四等一级帮办

21. 为汇报对经水路往来滨江关与瑷珲关之土货的征税办法进行调整事

DUTY TREATMENT: of native goods carried by river between Harbin and Aigun, etc.: Kuan-wu Shu's proposal re alteration of present procedure: Aigun Commissioner's views in the matter, submitted.

584

584
I.G.

I.G.

A I G U N 15th October 1931.

Sir,

1. I have the honour to acknowledge receipt of copy of I. G. despatch No. 4,552/137,395 to Harbin docketed :

> Duty Treatment: of native goods carried by river between Harbin and Aigun, and from inland places in the riverine district to Harbin: alteration of present procedure proposed by Kuan-wu Shu: I. G.'s instructions:

and in this connection to submit that the question of the duty treatment of cargo carried by steamer between Aigun and Harbin, or vice versa, is not affected by the instructions of Circular No. 4240 but is governed by the regulations contained in Circular No. 4236. It is presumed that the instructions of I. G. despatch No. 4,552/137,395 refer only to Harbin Customs intra-district riverine trade and that, in the event of the present practice of levying duty on native goods carried by vessels on the Sungari being abolished, it would still be necessary for this office to collect:-

(a) Interport duty on native goods carried by steamer to Lahasusu, to Harbin and to intermadiate points on the Sungari, and

(b) Interport duty on native goods carried by steamer to places on the Amur below Lahasusu and to places on the Ussuri as they would pass another Treaty Port (Lahasusu) en route. In practice, there are no such shipments.

2.

The Inspector General of Customs,

S H A N G H A I.

2. As will be seen from the Return of Non-urgent Chinese Correspondence for the month of September 1931, the Taheiho Chamber of Commerce petitioned the Heilungkiang Provincial Government, through the Heilungkiang General Chamber of Commerce, regarding the levy of Interport Duty by the Aigun Customs and that, in reply, I pointed out that this duty is levied in accordance with Government instructions.

I have the honour to be,

Sir,

Your obedient Servant,

(C. H. B. Joly)

Acting Commissioner.

呈海关总税务司署584号文　　　　　　　　　　　　瑷珲关1931年10月15日

尊敬的海关总税务司（上海）：

1. 根据海关总税务司署致滨江关第4552/137395号令：

“征税办法：关务署提议对经水路往来滨江关与瑷珲关，及自内地沿河各处运至滨江关之土货的现行征税办法进行调整；附海关总税务司署相关指示。”

兹汇报，经水路往来瑷珲关与滨江关之土货的征税办法，乃为海关总税务司署第4236号通令所辖之事，与第4240号通令之指示并无干系。而海关总税务司署致滨江关第4552/137395号令之指示，亦仅涉及滨江关辖区内的水路贸易。

如今，经水路往来松花江各处之土货的征税办法虽已废除，但瑷珲关仍需：

（1）对由轮船运至拉哈苏苏、滨江关及松花江沿岸其他各处之土货征收转口税；

（2）对由轮船运至黑龙江沿岸拉哈苏苏下游各处及乌苏里江沿岸各处之土货征收转口税，如此征税，乃因此等货物途中会经由另一通商口岸（拉哈苏苏），但实际上并无此等运输。

2. 如1931年9月非紧急中文往来函摘由簿所载，黑河商会已通过黑龙江总商会向黑龙江省政府就瑷珲关征收转口税一事提出抗议。对此，本署于回复中指出，转口税乃照政府指示征收。

您忠诚的仆人

周骊（C. H. B. Joly）

瑷珲关署理税务司

此抄件发送至滨江关税务司。

录事：陈培因　四等一级帮办

专题二

面、油、糖、酒、谷物、卷烟征税

1. 为商议避免对酒桶重复征税事

14.

I. G.

Aigun/Taheiho 7th December, 1921.

Sir,

I have the honour to enclose copy of a petition handed in by the firm of Wan Fu Kuang (萬福廣), owners of a large Spirit Factory at Fuliardi (富爾基), on the Railway between Tsitsihar and Manchuli. - The petitioners constantly carry spirit in drums to Taheiho, and the local practice, for which I cannot find authority, is to charge duty on the Spirit only on importation, and on the empty drums when they are shipped back to Fuliardi; the petitioners complain with reason that they are made to pay duty on drums every time they pass through the Customs, and they ask the Customs to devise means to avoid the repeated levy of duty.

I

The Inspector General of Customs,

PEKING.

I saw the representative of the firm, and I told him that the question would be referred to you; I suggest that they be allowed to engrave their marks and running numbers on all their drums as they arrive at Taheiho, under Customs supervision (which they are willing to do); duty should be collected at the time of marking, and the drums should be thereafter exempted from duty.

Pending the receipt of your instructions I intend, should the petitioners so request, to collect duty on deposit on such barrels as, having been duly marked and having paid duty once, shall pass this Custom House again.

I have the honour to be,

Sir,

Your obedient Servant,

G. Bochi.

Acting Commissioner.

A-27c]

No. 19. COMMRS.

Aigun. No. 87,330

Inspectorate General of Customs,

PEKING, 30th December, 1921.

SIR,

I am directed by the Inspector General to acknowledge receipt of your Despatch No. 14 :

enclosing copy of petition from the firm Wang Fu Kuang (萬福廣) owners of a large spirit factory at Fuliardi (富爾基), situated on the railway between Tsitsihar and Manchouli, complaining that they are made to pay duty on the drums containing the spirit every time they pass through the Customs, and requesting that means be devised to avoid the repeated levy of duty; stating that it is your local practice, for which you can find no authority, to charge duty on the spirit only on importation and on the empty drums when they are returned to Fuliardi and suggesting that the firm be permitted to engrave, under Customs supervision, their marks and running numbers on all their drums as they arrive at Taheiho, that duty should be collected at the time of marking and that the drums

thereafter

THE COMMISSIONER OF CUSTOMS,

A I G U N.

thereafter should be exempt from duty; and, in reply, to say that before he decides this question, the Inspector General wishes to be clearly informed why duty is levied on these goods at all - inwards or outwards. I am also to enquire if these goods pass the Liang-chia-t'un barrier ?

I am,

Sir,

Your obedient Servant,

Chief Secretary.

25.
I. G.

Aigun/Taheiho 2nd February, 22

Sir,

I have the honour to acknowledge the receipt of your despatch No. 19/87,330 :

calling for information on duty treatment of Spirit and Spirit Drums moved between Fuliardi (富爾基) and Taheiho:

and, in reply, to give the following explanations :

1. The Spirit imported overland from Fuliardi, and the empty Drums going back from Taheiho to Fuliardi, all pass the Liancgchiat'un Barrier.

2. Duty is levied on them, following the general principles on which the Liangchia-t'un Barrier is operated, viz :

a) Native Spirit, imported overland, is charged a full Export Duty, on the assumption that it is intended for export abroad;

b) Foreign Drums, imported overland, full of Spirit, should be taxed according to ~~practice~~ rules : the principle is, apparently, that

The Inspector General of Customs,

PEKING.

that duty is to be charged on <u>foreign goods</u>, brought into an open Port (or its Sub-Station) through a Customs Barrier, if they cannot produce proof of former payment of Duty. - The drums in question, however, have been passed free of duty for a long time, presumably because they have been considered as "packing" of the Spirit ;

c) Foreign Drums exported empty from Taheiho to Poliardi are charged one full Import Duty, because they may have been imported from abroad without our cognisance, and they show no proof of former payment.

The point of view expressed under a) is fully justified in this particular case, because the Spirit imported overland is locally turned into Vodka, and totally smuggled into Siberia. The contention under c) may not be correct in this particular instance, but the Customs have no formal way to ascertain the provenance of the barrels, unless a special arrangement is adopted, possibly on the lines indicated in Aigun despatch No. 14.

I

I have therefore the honour to request your sanction of my proposal to have the drums engraved under Customs supervision, charging one Import Duty once for all.

I have the honour to be,

Sir,

Your obedient Servant,

[signature]

Acting Commissioner.

4-27c]

No 28 . COMMRS. **Inspectorate General of Customs,**

Aigun No. 87,963. PEKING, 15th February, 1922.

SIR,

I am directed by the Inspector General to acknowledge receipt of your Despatch No. 25: (with reference to your despatch No. 14, and in reply to I. G. despatch No. 19/87,330):

reporting with regard to the duty treatment of spirit drums, that the spirit imported overland from Fuliardi and the empty drums going back from Taheiho to Fuliardi, all pass the Liangchiat'un Barrier; and that the principles on which duty is levied at this Barrier, are, viz:

(a) Native spirit, imported overland is charged a full export duty, on the assumption that it is intended for export abroad;

(b) Foreign drums, imported overland, full of spirit, have been passed free of duty presumably because they have been considered as "packing" of the spirit; and

(c)

THE COMMISSIONER OF CUSTOMS,

AIGUN.

(c) Foreign drums, exported empty from Taheiho to Fuliardi, are charged one full Import Duty, because they may have been imported from abroad without our cognisance, and they show no proof of former payment;

stating that the point of view expressed under (a) is fully justified in this particular case, because the spirit imported overland is locally turned into Vodka and smuggled into Siberia; but that the contention under (c) may not be correct in this particular instance as the Customs have no way to ascertain the provenance of the barrels unless a special arrangement is adopted, and, therefore, requesting sanction to have the drums engraved under Customs supervision, and charging one Import Duty once for all;

and, in reply, to say that the drums having once paid duty and having been engraved in a way that makes each drum easily identifiable may, thereafter, be allowed to pass

to

to and fro without further payment.

I am,

Sir,

Your obedient Servant,

Chief Secretary.

No. 36 Service

Aigun. No. 840.

CUSTOM HOUSE,

Harbin, 29th May, 1923.

Sir,

I have to acknowledge receipt of your despatch No. 35,

Drums, Spirit: marked and numbered at Taheiho: proposal to pass free of further duty when moved on Amur and Sungari, submitting.

and, in reply, to inform you that the offices in the Harbin District will be instructed to pass these drums free of duty.

This practice will no doubt give rise to further registration of drums at Aigun, and I propose to leave this work entirely in the hands of your office, the Harbin Customs levying duty on all drums which have not been marked, or the marking of which has not been notified by Aigun.

I will request you to notify the Sungari offices, i. e. Harbin Central Custom House, Lahasusu and

To

The Commissioner of Customs.

A I G U N.

and Sansing, direct by General Office Memo. when further lots of drums are marked and numbered by your Office.

I am,

Sir,

Your obedient Servant,

Commissioner.

呈海关总税务司署 14 号文　　　　　　　　　　瑷珲关 / 大黑河 1921 年 12 月 7 日

尊敬的海关总税务司(北京):

兹附万福广商行请愿书抄件一份。该商行位于齐齐哈尔至满洲里铁路沿线,并于富尔基[①]建有一家大型酿酒厂,一直将酒盛于酒桶内运至大黑河。按照惯例(该惯例之授权并未寻得),此酒进入大黑河时,瑷珲关仅对酒征税,待其返回富尔基时,再对空桶征税。然该商行抱怨称,每次过关皆须缴纳酒桶税,希望海关采取措施,避免重复征税。

本署已面见该商行代表,并告知此事将提请海关总税务司署裁定。兹提议,准许该商行在海关的监管下,于酒水抵达大黑河后,将商行之标志及流水号码刻于所有酒桶之上(商行亦同意此法);海关可于标记之时对酒桶征税,待其返回时则可予以免税放行。

兹计划,凡该商行之酒桶已标记并完税一次者,再次通过海关时,暂以押金之形式缴纳税款,待贵署予以进一步指示后,再做处置。

您忠诚的仆人

包安济(G. Boezi)

瑷珲关署理税务司

① 富尔基(Fulisrdi)乃为档案原文给定,据查应为今富拉尔基,是齐齐哈尔市一个市辖区,区中心位于齐齐哈尔市西南 37 公里处。

致瑷珲关第 19/87330 号令　　　　海关总税务司署（北京）1921 年 12 月 30 日

尊敬的瑷珲关税务司：

第 14 号呈收悉：

“随函附上齐齐哈尔至满洲里铁路上富尔基大型酒厂老板万福广的请愿书，其大意是申诉每次过关时都必须对酒桶缴税，并请求对这种方法加以修改，以免重复征税；指出对进口时的酒及运回富尔基的空桶征收关税是瑷珲关独有的做法，实际并没有得到相关授权，并建议准许该公司抵达大黑河关后在海关的监管下，在其所有酒桶上刻上他们的标志和流水号码，关税则在做标记之时征收，自此之后酒桶应予以免税。”

奉总税务司命令，现批复如下：总税务司希望在其决定如何处理该问题之前，清楚地了解为什么要在入境和出境时对这些货物征税。另外，我想了解这些货物是否会通过梁家屯分卡。

您忠诚的仆人

包罗（C. A. V. Bowra）

总务科税务司

呈海关总税务司署25号文　　　　瑷珲关/大黑河1922年2月2日

尊敬的海关总税务司（北京）：

根据海关总税务司署第19/87300号令：

“请汇报瑷珲关对往来富尔基与大黑河之间的酒及酒桶的征税办法。”

兹汇报如下。

1. 无论是自富尔基经陆路运入大黑河之酒，还是由大黑河返回富尔基之空酒桶，途中均须经由梁家屯分卡。

2. 梁家屯分卡对酒及酒桶的征税办法如下：

（1）凡经由陆路进口之土酒，均按出口至国外的货物办理，对之征收出口正税；

（2）凡经由陆路进口之洋酒桶（满载），若照规定，“凡洋货前往通商口岸（或分关）者，若无完税凭证，沿途海关分卡将对之征税”，理应征税，然因此酒桶乃为装酒容器，故一直未对之征税；

（3）凡由大黑河出口至富尔基之空洋酒桶，因无完税凭证，又无法查证是否为自国外进口，故一律征收进口正税。

于此事而言，（1）项办法十分合理，因经由陆路进口之酒最终会于当地制成伏特加，而后走私至西伯利亚，而（3）项办法或有不合理之处，但海关若不采取特殊办法，实难通过正式途径探查酒桶之来源。故特此申请按照瑷珲关第14号呈所述办法，准许商行在海关的监管下，为酒桶刻上标记，由海关于标记之时对酒桶征收一次性进口正税。

您忠诚的仆人

包安济（G. Boezi）

瑷珲关署理税务司

致瑷珲关第28/87963号令　　　　海关总税务司署（北京）1922年2月15日

尊敬的瑷珲关税务司：

第25号呈收悉（根据瑷珲关第14号呈及对海关总税务司署第19/87330号令的回复）：

"汇报关于酒桶的征税办法，经由陆路从富尔基进口的烈酒和从大黑河运送回富尔基的空桶都需要通过梁家屯分卡。"

本分卡对此类货物的课税原则如下：

（1）凡经由陆路进口且拟出口到国外的土酒，一律征收出口正税；

（2）凡经由陆路进口且装满酒的洋酒桶，一律免税放行，因为酒桶可视为烈酒的"包装物"；以及

（3）凡从大黑河出口至富尔基的空洋酒桶，一律征收进口正税，因为其无法出示先前的缴税凭证，我们无从知晓它们是不是从国外进口的酒桶。

说明第（1）条中的观点在此特定情形下完全合理，因为经由陆地进口的烈酒在这一带被调制成伏特加酒，进而走私到西伯利亚；但第（3）条中的主张在此情形中并不正确，因为除非采取特殊安排，否则海关无法探查酒桶的来源，因此，请您批准在海关的监督下给酒桶刻上标记，并一次性征收出口税。

奉总税务司命令，现批复如下：兹告知，凡缴纳一次性税并刻了易识别标记的酒桶，其后出入境均无须另外缴税。

您忠诚的仆人

包罗（C. A. V. Bowra）

总务科税务司

致瑷珲关第36/840号函　　　　　　　　　　　　哈尔滨关1923年5月29日

尊敬的瑷珲关税务司：

根据瑷珲关致哈尔滨关第35号函：

“酒桶：提议凡酒桶于大黑河标记编号后，往来黑龙江和松花江时，均予免税放行。”

兹告知，本署将指示哈尔滨关区各分卡对此等酒桶免税放行。

只是如此一来，日后至瑷珲关为酒桶登记者势必会更多，有鉴于此，兹提议，由贵署全权负责标记之事，哈尔滨关则相应对所有未标记或未经瑷珲关通知已标记之酒桶征税。

瑷珲关日后为酒桶标记编号后，还请以征税汇办处备忘录之形式告知松花江沿岸各关，即哈尔滨关、拉哈苏苏分关及三姓分关。

您忠诚的仆人

（签字）覃书（R. C. L. d' Anjou）

哈尔滨关税务司

2. 为禁止黑龙江省小麦出口的相关指示事

39 COMMRS.

Aigun No. 88,948

INSPECTORATE GENERAL OF CUSTOMS,

PEKING, 13th April, 1922.

Sir,

I append, for your information and guidance, copy of Shui-wu Ch'u despatch No. 503, from which you will see that the export of wheat from the Heilungkiang Province has been temporarily prohibited and that you are to consult with the Taoyin and Superintendent and to notify the public accordingly, allowing the usual period of three weeks from date of notification before the prohibition is carried into effect.

You are requested to act accordingly.

I am,

Sir,

Your obedient Servant,

F. Aglen

Inspector General.

The Commissioner of Customs,

AIGUN.

I.G.despatch No. 39 to Aigun,

Appendix No.1.

稅務處令第五〇三號 中華民國十一年四月十日

案准黑龍江督軍電開據黑河道尹電稱禁運小麥一案去冬十一月電奉令准通知各國領事在案現愛琿海關仍准俄商購運小麥以未奉稅務處令知未便照辦擬請電咨轉飭照辦以維民食等情查該處上年小麥歉收電請本署禁運當經照准並令查照禁運辦法如有先期買定者限二十一日以內發照運出復於十一月二十二日令行特派交涉員通知各國領事查照在案據電前情應請迅飭該關遵照辦理並希電復等因前來除電復黑龍江督軍並分行外相應令行總稅務司查照轉令愛琿關稅務司會商該關監督及黑河道尹先期出示暫行禁運可也此令

袁振華
陳書鈦 同校

致瑷珲关第 39/88948 号令　　　　海关总税务司署（北京）1922 年 4 月 13 日

尊敬的瑷珲关税务司：

为了便于贵署顺利执行，兹附中方税务处第 503 号令，以供参考。据该令所示，已暂时禁止黑龙江省小麦出口，您需与道尹和海关监督一同商议此事，并且通知民众，自通知之日起，留出三周的宽限期，禁令方可生效。

敬请遵照此令执行。

您忠诚的仆人

安格联（F. A. Aglen）

海关总税务司

3. 为黑龙江省小麦出口已禁止及海关有关告示现可发布事

51 COMMRS.

INSPECTORATE GENERAL OF CUSTOMS,

No. 89,796

PEKING, 13th June, 1922.

Sir,

With reference to my despatch No. 39/88,948: Wheat: export of, from Heilungkiang Province, prohibited: instructions;

I append, for your information and guidance, copy of Shui-wu Ch'u despatch No. 810, from which you will see that this question has been the subject of further correspondence between the Heilungkiang Tuchün and the Shui-wu Ch'u, and between the Shui-wu Ch'u and myself. The Heiho Taoyin reported that, in view of the provincial prohibition proclaimed in November, 1921, the issue of a Customs Notification allowing export of wheat contracted for before the 21st May, 1922, would cause misunderstanding on the part of local merchants and requested that you be instructed not to issue any notification. I explained in reply that export of wheat to Siberia is allowed under special treaty stipulations and

Commissioner of Customs,

AIGUN.

and the Commissioners cannot act upon provincial authorities' notification for suspension of this privilege as in the case of prohibition of export of grain from one province to another, and that, as the Aigun Customs does not appear to have as yet prohibited export of grain, the non-issuance of a Customs notification as requested by the Taoyin would only have the effect of continuing to allow export of grain. The Shui-wu Ch'u concurs and instructs that you are now to issue the notification, in consultation with the Superintendent, allowing the usual period of three weeks before the prohibition is enforced.

You are requested to act accordingly.

I am,

Sir,

Your obedient Servant,

F. Aglen

Inspector General.

I.G.Despatch No. 51 to Aigun,

Appendix No.1.

稅務處令第八一〇號

中華民國十一年六月八日

案查本年四月間准黑龍江督軍來電以據黑河道尹電稱禁運小麥一案去冬通知各國領事在案現愛琿海關仍准俄商購運小麥以未奉稅務處令知未便照辦等情懇請迅飭該關遵辦等因當經本處於是月十日分令遵辦並電復黑龍江督軍各在案嗣據愛琿關監督代電稱奉令咨准愛琿關稅務司復稱應由本年五月一日起至二十一日止限商民先期購定小麥者運出口岸等語查小麥禁運一案限於去冬十一月二十二日起至十二月十三日止凡先期買定小麥者准其運出早經佈告並通知各國領事迄今數月仍在厲行禁運之期若照該稅務司所言名爲限期准運實則不啻弛禁與前案未免抵觸且恐地方商民誤會激生事端乃再四磋商該稅務司雖亦諒解然終以與令不符爲疑只允暫緩佈告由該監督請示遵辦惟有懇請飭令總稅務司轉飭愛琿關稅務司解除誤會將本年五月一日至二十一日限期佈告不再張貼以維民食等情復經本處以黑河地方小麥禁運出口既經黑河道尹於去冬早經佈告並通知各國領事且現在厲行禁運之期自可無

庸由愛琿關再行張貼告示以免商民有所誤會令行總稅務司轉令該關稅務司遵照去後茲據總稅務司呈稱查尋常禁運米穀出口按照一九〇二年中英條約第十四款規定辦法如中國地方官憲先於二十一日前出示禁止米穀等糧由該通商口岸運往中國通商別口所有各口海關自應一律遵照辦理曾由總稅務司通令行知各關稅務司知照在案惟此次黑河道尹禁運小麥出口一事係禁止小麥由愛琿運往俄國核與尋常禁止米穀由中國通商某口運往中國通商別口情形並不相同在愛琿關稅務司未奉總稅務司明令自無權但憑道尹所出告示即行禁止小麥出口溯查中俄條約俄商似可由愛琿購買小麥出口運往俄國並因最惠國條款各該他國商人亦可按照辦理蓋前項中俄條約似無禁止米穀等糧出口之條文如果中國政府意欲禁止出運應行特別出示方爲正辦職是之故愛琿關稅務司對於黑河道尹去冬禁運小麥出口一案未允按照道尹所出告示辦理堅持須遵照中央政府飭由總稅務司轉行該關令文另行張貼禁運佈告限自五月一日起至二十一日止准商民將先期購定之小麥運出口岸總稅務司竊以該關稅務

司如此辦理尚屬妥適緣在愛琿海關迄今並未禁止小麥報運出口是以非由關張貼禁運告示則商民等自仍可將該口小麥繼續輸運出境是否有當理合呈請鑒核施行等因前來本處復查此事既據總稅務司呈復前因是愛琿海關迄今並未禁止小麥出口應即由愛琿關監督會同該關稅務司將前項禁運小麥出口日期另行訂定先期出示佈告俾資遵守而重民食除分行外相應令行總稅務司查照迅即轉令愛琿關稅務司遵照會同該關監督妥爲辦理此令

袁振華
趙學謙 仝校

致瑷珲关第 51/89796 号令　　　　海关总税务司署（北京）1922 年 6 月 13 日

尊敬的瑷珲关税务司：

根据第 39/88948 号令：

"黑龙江省小麦出口已禁止；相关指示。"

为了便于贵署顺利执行，兹附税务处第 810 号令副本，以供参考。据该令所示，黑龙江督军与税务处、税务处与海关总税务司署之间的往来通信已商讨此事。黑河道尹报告，鉴于 1921 年 11 月已颁布全省禁令，海关所发 1922 年 5 月 21 日前先期签约的小麦允许出口的告示会引发当地商民误解，故贵署不应颁布任何相关告示。在回复中本署解释，由于向西伯利亚出口小麦另有专门条约规定，在省政府发布取消省之间出口谷物特权的告示之后，瑷珲关税务司无法按照禁止谷物从一省出口到他省的规定情形执行禁运。而且，瑷珲关目前尚未禁止出口谷物，由于应道尹要求海关告示并未发布，只能继续允许谷物出口。税务处表示认同，并指示贵署现可在与海关监督商议后发布告示，在执行禁令前照常留出三周宽限期。

敬请遵照此令执行。

您忠诚的仆人

安格联（F. A. Aglen）

海关总税务司

4. 为申请批准于取消特别减税及免税优惠后开始对出口小麦及面粉征税事

60.

, G.

Aigun / Taheiho 27th June, 1922.

Sir,

1. I have the honour to report that, when I received your instructions that the Duty Free List was to be abolished from 1st April, 1922, I consulted with the Harbin Commissioner on the practical application of the Tariff from that date, and that, inter alia, we agreed that flour exported abroad should be dutiable. I accordingly ordered duty to be charged since 1st April. - But, on 20th instant, the Superintendent communicated a petition from the Heiho Chamber of Commerce, stating that exportation abroad of flour from Harbin is allowed free of duty (in support of which contention they produce telegrams of the Harbin and Manchouli Chambers of Commerce), and that the Customs Duty is a very heavy burden on Flour in these times of stagnant trade; asking that

for

Inspector General of Customs,

P E K I N G.

for these reasons no duty be charged in future, and that duty already collected be refunded.

2. This question was thouroughly reported by Mr. Anjou in Harbin despatch No. 2289 of 1920. The principal objection then made by the Shui Wu Ch'u and Wai-chiaoPu to levy of duty (your despatch No. 2475/82,622) was based on the existence of Treaties and Special Agreements with Russia. - Seeing that these have now been abolished, and that export abroad by water is allowed on payment of duty at Newchwang, Dairen and Antung, and of payment of special fee at Shanghai, Hankow and Tientsin (Memorandum appended to your despatch No. 2475/82,622)there appears to be no reason to pass free of duty flour exported abroad from this port, by River or across the River. Were it not for the fear that the Ch'u may be approached by the local merchants or Authorities, and the case misrepresented, I would not develop further arguments in favour of levy of duty.

3. The report of the Chambers of Commerce at Harbin and Manchouli that flour exported abroad from those places is passed free, is probably due to the

fact,

fact, of which I am semi-officially informed, that in Harbin Duty is collected on exportation of Flour by River, while flour exported by Railway is still passed free; the reason is that, whereas the Overland Trade Regulations attached to the 1881 Petersburg Treaty have ceased to be enforced as from 1st April, the stipulations regarding the reduced Duty Payment mentioned in the "Contrat pour la Construction et Exploitation du Chemin de Fer de l'Est" (1896) still hold good, and consequently the provisional Regulations of the Agreement between Customs and Railway (1908), still affect railway traffic.

4. The Chamber of Commerce's statement that a 5% duty is too heavy a burden on Flour Trade, is preposterous. Mr. d'Anjou has already stated the plain facts of the case in his despatch No. 2289, § 7; what he has said of the Harbin District is strictly true of the Aigun District now. The general lull in trade has not in the least affected export abroad of flour - our statistics speaks for themselves : in April 1922, 1,500 pls. were exported, worth Hk. Tls. 9,194; in May, 10,776 pls., value

Hk. Tls.

Hk. Tls. 72,576; from 1st to 20th June, pls. 18,826, value Hk. Tls. 118,579 ; total pls. 31,102, value Hk. Tls. 200,349. The exportation continues, and much flour is exported clandestinely above Harbour limits, or declared for the Chinese side of the River and then carried across to the Russian side, thus avoiding payment of duty. - The huge profits realised by the local Flour Mills are also shown by the maximum prices fixed by the local Magistrate at the end of March, which ruled until quite recently : Flour II, per pood, $ 3.50; III grade, $ 3.30; IV grade, $ 2.80. - Besides, the Mills are greatly favoured by the prohibition to export wheat, which has been long and effectively enforced by the Local Tax Office before Shui Wu Ch'u sanction, and which is all for the benefit of the Mills and the Spirit Factories, as the Russians cannot mill Flour or make Vodka in Blagovestchensk out of Chinese wheat, and are obliged to buy in Taheiho.

5. Finally I would point out that the duty is actually paid by the Russians; and, as the flour exported abroad from this Port is almost exclusively

for

for use of the Military, I hope that the Customs will not be asked to sacrifice a good and legitimate Revenue for the benefit of the Army of the Far Eastern Republic.

6. These facts and arguments I have quoted in my reply to the Superintendent; my reply, together with the Superintendent's original communication, is appended.

字一百九十三號

字四十七號

As this question may interest Harbin as well as this Office, copy of this despatch is being forwarded to the Harbin Commissioner.

I have the honour to be,

Sir,

Your obedient Servant,

G. Boon

Acting Commissioner.

2 1922

Harbin Commissioner's comments on Aigun Despatch No. 60/ I.G. of 27th June, 1922.

In February this year, after the receipt of I. G. instructions concerning the abolition of the one-third duty reduction and duty free list (Circular No.3252, II), my opinion was sought by Mr G. Boezi, Acting Commissioner, on the following points:

a) Duty treatment of Manchurian wheat flour when exported abroad.

b) What is the Shanghai practice ?

c) Will it be necessary to issue a special notification to the public concerning the dutiability of flour when exported abroad after 31st March, 1922 ?

and the gist of my reply is as follows:

a) Manchurian wheat flour will be liable to export duty on 1st April. The export abroad of Manchurian-grown wheat flour from Antung, Dairen and Newchwang is allowed on payment of duty (5% ad valorem) according to I. G. Circular No. 2457. Flour from other parts of China is not allowed to be exported abroad (based on I.G. Circular No.1786); in fact flour should not have been allowed to be exported to Russia via Suifenho, Manchouli, Lahasusu and Aigun, but it has become an established practice in this district and for this privilege it is reasonable to demand payment of an export duty. I have instructed my

stations

stations to collect duty from 1st April.

b) The Shanghai practice is to allow exportation abroad of foreign machine-milled native flour under Huchao issued by the Superintendent of Customs. Whether or not it is allowed to go free of export duty, I cannot say.

c) I do not consider it necessary to issue a special notification to the public if you have already issued a general notification concerning the abolition of the duty reduction and duty free list. It appears to me inadvisable to raise the question whether or not flour becomes dutiable after 31st March, but to take it for granted that it does in the spirit of the new Circular instructions (Circular No. 3252, II).

Acting upon this advice the Aigun Commissioner started collection of duty on flour exported across to Russia. Why Manchurian flour was allowed to go free of duty on exportation to Russia from the Harbin River Customs and Sungari stations since the 1st April contrary to my intentions is a matter which I have been endeavouring to clear up without success. Were my verbal instructions misunderstood or forgotten in the rush of work at the opening of the navigation season I am at a loss to explain. The fact remains however that while the abolition of the one-third duty reduction and the special duty free privileges on beans, cereals and firewood shipped on the Sungari was carried into effect

effect from the 1st April, flour continued to be passed free on export abroad from the Sungari ports and it was not until the Aigun Commissioner called my attention to the fact that I realised that my intention had miscarried.

But if my contentions are accepted by the Inspector General that Manchurian flour became dutiable on exportation abroad from the 1st April, as is the case at Antung, Dairen and Newchwang, the matter can be easily remedied by a Notification to the public giving, if necessary, one or two months notice. The Flour trade with Russia can easily bear a taxation of 5% ad valorem on exportation and the fact that Aigun has been charging duty since 1st April is a strong factor in our favour.

Commissioner.

Custom House,

Harbin, 15th July, 1922.

呈海关总税务司署60号文　　　　　　　　瑷珲关/大黑河 1922年6月27日

尊敬的海关总税务司（北京）：

1. 兹报告，在收到海关总税务司署关于自1922年4月1日起取消满洲北方陆地边界特别减税及免税优惠之指令[①]后，本署便与哈尔滨关税务司商议新的征税办法，最后商定对出口至国外的面粉征税。随后，本署便下令自4月1日起开始征收此税，然6月20日又收到由海关监督代转之黑河商会请愿书一封，请愿书中指出目前哈尔滨关对出口至国外的面粉均予免税放行（黑河商会为此特附上哈尔滨及满洲里商会的相关电报），并言时下贸易如此萧条，海关对出口国外之面粉所征税率实在过高，于面粉贸易而言负担过重，故请求不再征税，并退还已纳税款。

2. 哈尔滨关税务司覃书（R.C.L.d'Anjou）先生于1920年哈尔滨关第2289号呈中便已经详尽汇报过对面粉征税之事。当时税务处及外交部反对征收此税（参阅海关总税务司署第2475/82622号令）主要碍于中俄签订之条约及特殊协定。然如今特别减税及免税优惠既已取消，而且牛庄关、大连关、安东关均对经水运出口至国外的面粉征收关税，江海关、江汉关及津海关亦对此类面粉收取税费（参阅海关总税务司署第2475/82622号令所附备忘录），有鉴于此，瑷珲关并无理由对经水运出口至国外的面粉免税放行。为避免当地商人及政府会向税务处申诉此事，造成误解，本署将进一步说明此项征税之理据。

3. 关于哈尔滨及满洲里商会声称当地出口至国外之面粉均获免税放行一事，兹认为，如本署私下所知，或因哈尔滨关仅对经水运出口之面粉征税，而对经铁路出口之面粉依然免税放行；毕竟自4月1日起，1881年《圣彼得堡条约》附属之《中俄陆路通商章程》虽已废止，但1896年中俄《合办东省铁路公司合同章程》关于减免关税之规定仍然有效，而且铁路运输仍受海关与铁路局1908年所签协议中的暂行规定影响。

4. 至于商会认为海关值百抽五之税率于面粉贸易而言负担过重，实在荒谬。哈尔滨关税务司覃书先生早已于哈尔滨关第2289号呈中对面粉出口之事予以说明，而瑷珲关目前之状况更是如此。瑷珲关各项数据表明，面粉向国外出口之事并未受到贸易整体停滞之影响。1922年4月，出口至国外的面粉量达1500担，价值9194海关两；5月10776担，价值72576海关两；6月1日至20日18826担，价值118579海关两；总计31102担，价值200349海关两。面粉出口还在继续，而且其中大量面粉皆为自港口界限以外暗中出

① 参考《旧中国海关总税务司署通令选编》（第二卷），海关总税务司署通令第3252号（第二辑）。

口，或于报关时申报运往黑龙江华岸各地，再自他处跨江运至俄岸，以便逃税。此外，当地县长于三月底对面粉所定价格为历来最高，且该价格一直延用至今，其中二等面粉每普特3.50银圆，三等面粉每普特3.30银圆；四等面粉每普特2.80银圆。由此可知，当地面粉厂皆已赚得暴利。另在税务处批准之前，税捐局一直禁止小麦出口，致使布拉戈维申斯克地区无法自磨面粉、自酿伏特加，只得自大黑河进口，本地面粉厂及酒厂亦因此而获利匪浅。

5. 最后，本署需指出，俄国人亦为此等面粉缴纳关税；而且自本口岸出口之面粉几乎仅为军用，望不要为远东共和国之利益而牺牲海关的合法税收。

6. 本署已将上述各项载于致海关监督的回函之中；兹附本署回函（监去字四十七号）及海关监督最初来函（监来字一百九十三号）。

鉴于此事亦涉及哈尔滨关，此抄件已发送至哈尔滨关税务司。

您忠诚的仆人

包安济（G. Boezi）

瑷珲关署理税务司

关于瑷珲关致海关总税务司署第60号呈的意见

海关总税务司署关于取消满洲北方陆地边界特别减税及免税优惠之通令第3252号（第二辑）下发后，瑷珲关署理税务司包安济（G.Boezi）先生便就以下几点与本署进行商议：

（1）满洲面粉出口至国外时应如何征税？

（2）江海关对此等面粉一向如何征税？

（3）是否需要发布专项公告，告知公众凡面粉于1922年3月31日以后出口至国外者，均须缴税？

本署回复要点如下：

（1）满洲面粉应自4月1日起完纳出口税。安东关、大连关及牛庄关目前均照海关总税务司署第2457号通令指示对产自满洲且出口国外之面粉按值百抽五之税率征收出口税；而中国其他地区所产面粉均须照海关总税务司署第1786号通令指示不得出口至国外；虽然面粉本不应获准经绥芬河、满洲里、拉哈苏苏及瑷珲出口至俄国，但该项出口既已成为当地惯例，相应地征收出口税亦十分合理。本署已命哈尔滨关各分关自4月1日起征收此项关税。

（2）按照江海关的惯例，由洋机器所研磨之土产面粉可持海关监督签发之护照出口至国外，至于是否免征出口税，本署尚不确定。

（3）若瑷珲关早已发布取消特别减税及免税优惠之公告，本署认为无须另行发布专项公告，更不宜提出是否应于3月31日后开始对面粉征税之事，唯谨遵海关总税务司署第3252号通令（第二辑）的指示精神办理即可。

瑷珲关税务司随后便根据此建议开始向出口至俄国的面粉征税。至于为何哈尔滨江关及松花江沿线各分关4月1日以后仍对出口至俄国的满洲面粉免税放行，本署亦十分困惑，业已竭力查证，但至今未果，不知是否因航运季伊始公务繁忙，各分关对本署口头传达之指令理解有误或是已经忘记。实际上，自4月1日起松花江上运输的豆类、谷类及木柈便开始遵照指令不再享有减税（三分减一）及免税优惠，唯有面粉仍享有自松花江各口免税出口国外之待遇，若非瑷珲关税务司报告，本署还不知晓此前所下达之命令竟未被遵照执行。

但总税务司若同意哈尔滨关自4月1日起与安东关、大连关及牛庄关一样向出口至国外的满洲面粉征税，本署则只需重新发布公告即可，如有必要，可持续公示 1 至 2 个月。此外，值百抽五之税率于满洲面粉出口贸易而言，绝非重负，而且瑷珲关已于4月 1 日起开始征收此税，足以证明该项征税办法切实可行。

章书（R.C.L.d'Anjou）

哈尔滨关税务司

1922 年 7 月 15 日，哈尔滨关

5. 为告知黑龙江省小麦出口禁令已撤销事

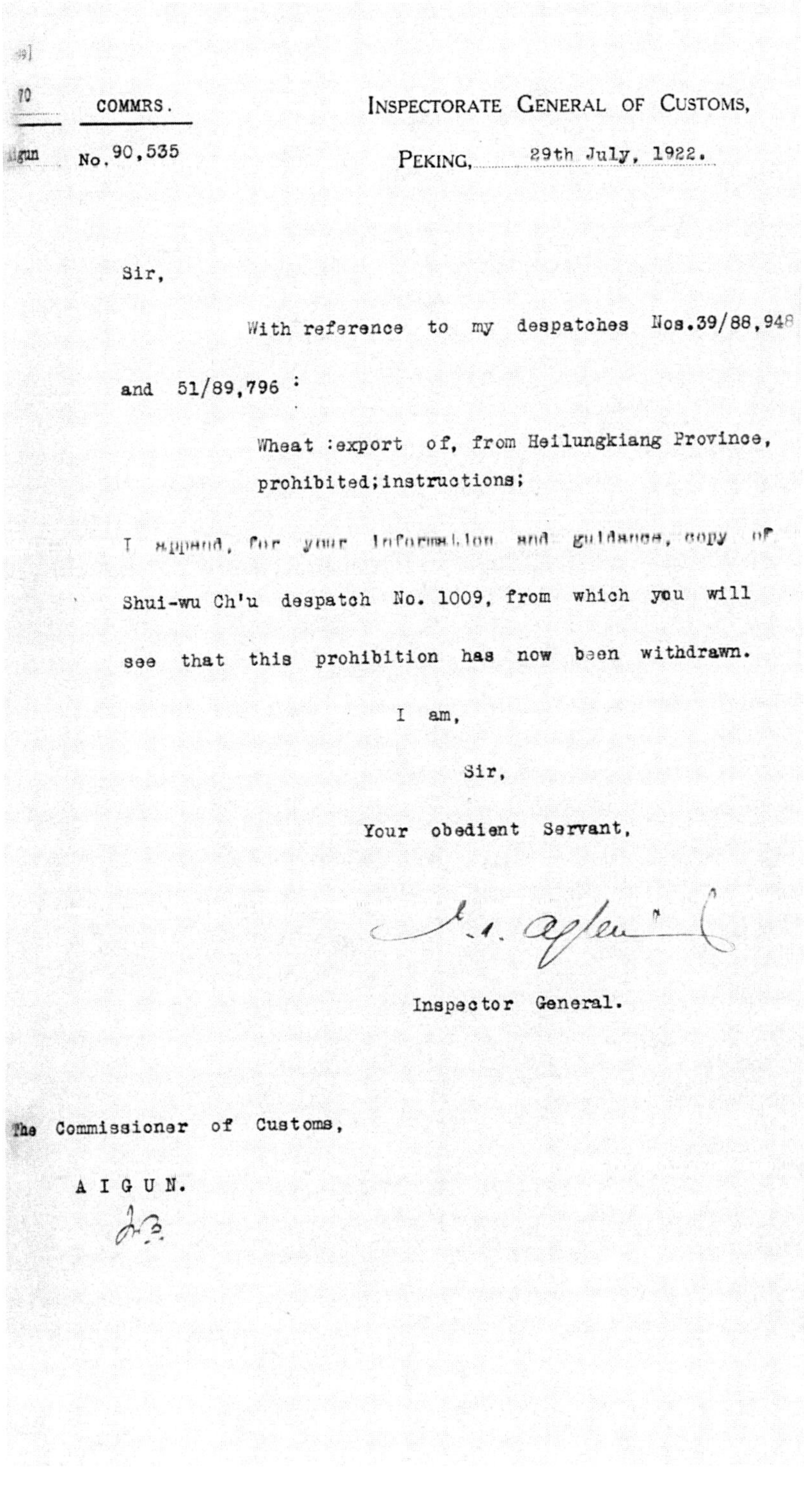

COMMRS.

INSPECTORATE GENERAL OF CUSTOMS,

Aigun No. 90,535

PEKING, 29th July, 1922.

Sir,

With reference to my despatches Nos.39/88,948 and 51/89,796 :

Wheat :export of, from Heilungkiang Province, prohibited;instructions;

I append, for your information and guidance, copy of Shui-wu Ch'u despatch No. 1009, from which you will see that this prohibition has now been withdrawn.

I am,

Sir,

Your obedient Servant,

F. A. Aglen

Inspector General.

The Commissioner of Customs,

AIGUN.

I.G.despatch No. 70 to Aigun,

Appendix No.1.

稅務處令第一〇〇九號 中華民國十一年七月二十七日

准黑龍江省長咨開據黑河道尹宋文郁電稱禁運小麥一案前經電奉令准茲據愛琿縣呈稱據農商各會呈稱現在雨暘時若麥收已有把握兼航路通行米糧紛集請即日將禁運一案速除以免日後穀賤傷農等情查核委係實情擬請照准并訂於七月十五日弛禁除佈告外理合電請分別行知各國領事暨稅務處查照等情除電復該道照辦并分別咨行外應咨行查照施行等因前來本處查愛琿縣所產小麥暫行禁運出口一事前准黑龍江省長來電當經本處於本年第五〇三號暨七六三等號令先後行知總稅務司轉令愛琿關稅務司遵辦在案茲復准黑龍江省長咨開前因除分行外相應令行總稅務司查照迅令愛琿關稅務司遵照可也此令

袁振華 同校
周啓明

致瑷珲关第70/90535号令　　　　海关总税务司署（北京）1922年7月29日

尊敬的瑷珲关税务司：

根据第39/88948号及第51/89796号令：

"黑龙江省小麦出口已禁止；相关指示。"

为了便于贵署顺利执行，兹附中方税务处第1009号令，以供参考。据该令所示，该禁令已撤消。特此告知。

您忠诚的仆人

安格联（Francis Arthur Aglen）

海关总税务司

6. 为对1922年4月1日至10月15日期间出口至国外的面粉所征关税进行退税事

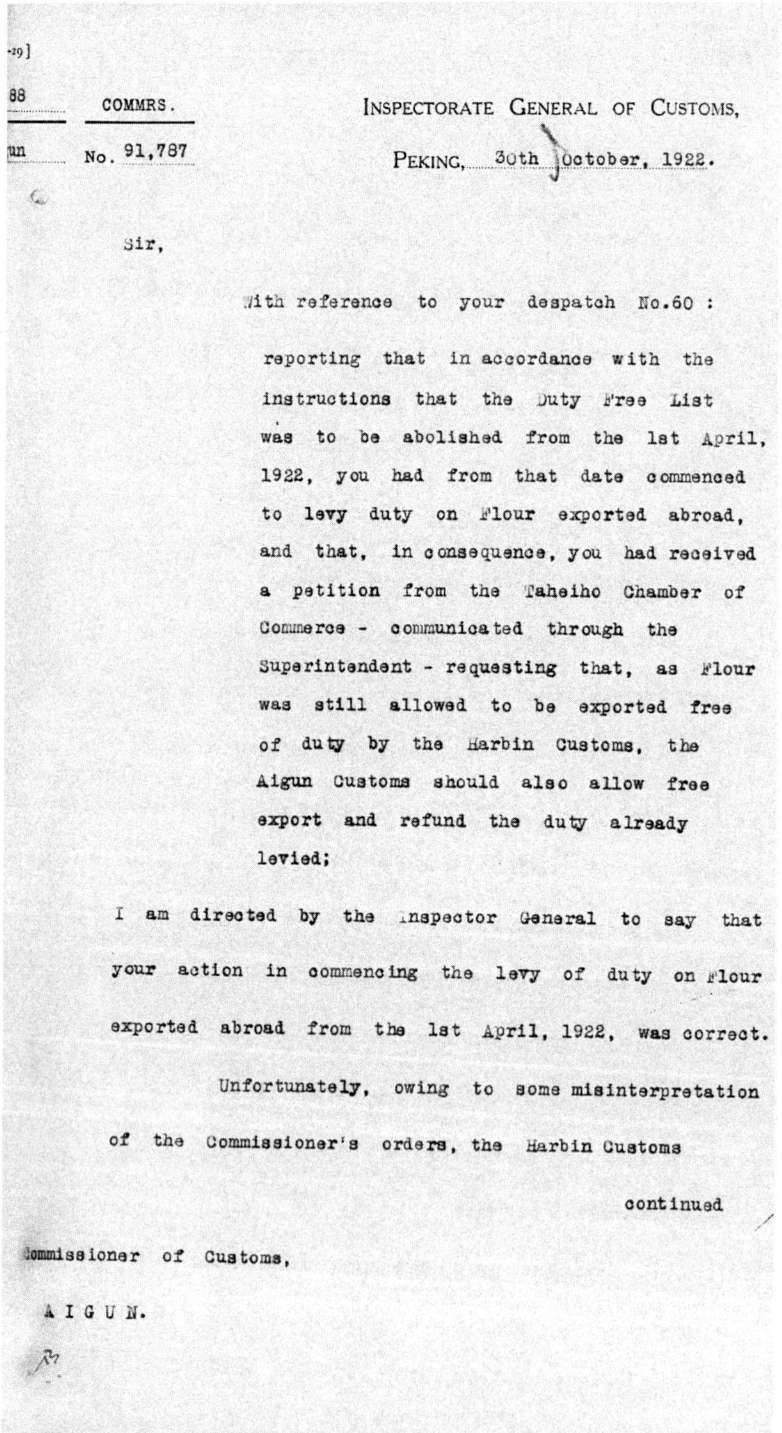

-29]

88 COMMRS.

un No. 91,787

INSPECTORATE GENERAL OF CUSTOMS,

PEKING, 30th October, 1922.

Sir,

With reference to your despatch No.60 :

reporting that in accordance with the instructions that the Duty Free List was to be abolished from the 1st April, 1922, you had from that date commenced to levy duty on Flour exported abroad, and that, in consequence, you had received a petition from the Taheiho Chamber of Commerce - communicated through the Superintendent - requesting that, as Flour was still allowed to be exported free of duty by the Harbin Customs, the Aigun Customs should also allow free export and refund the duty already levied;

I am directed by the Inspector General to say that your action in commencing the levy of duty on Flour exported abroad from the 1st April, 1922, was correct.

Unfortunately, owing to some misinterpretation of the Commissioner's orders, the Harbin Customs

continued

Commissioner of Customs,

AIGUN.

continued to allow Flour to be exported free after the 1st April, 1922, and the omission to levy duty was not brought to the Commissioner's attention until he received a copy of your despatch No.60 to the Inspector General - forwarded to him by yourself.

Owing to the existence of an arrangement with the Japanese Legation to the effect that rail-borne Flour exported from Antung should be subject to the same duty treatment as North Manchurian Flour exported by rail, it became necessary to refer the matter of the duty treatment of North Manchurian Flour to the Chinese Government. The Shui-wu Ch'u eventually ruled that Flour exported through the Custom Houses in North Manchuria - and therefore also Flour exported by rail from Antung - was to pay duty as from the 16th October, 1922.

From the appended copy of correspondence with the Shui-wu Ch'u you will see that the Flour

merchants

merchants in your district have petitioned that the duty paid on Flour exported at Aigun prior to the date on which Flour became dutiable at Harbin should be refunded, and that it has been decided to grant their petition.

Duty collected by your office on Flour during the period 1st April to 15th October, 1922, inclusive, may therefore be refunded.

I am,

Sir,

Your obedient Servant,

(signed) [illegible]

Chief Secretary.

3[A.—29]

No. 102 COMMRS.

Aigun No. 92,617

INSPECTORATE GENERAL OF CUSTOMS,

PEKING, 8th January 1923.

Sir,

With reference to I. G. despatch No. 88/91,787:

Flour (Wheat): Duty collected at Aigun from 1st April to 15th October 1922 to be refunded:

I am directed by the Inspector General to append copy of Shui-wu Ch'u despatch No. 1768 and its enclosure, from which you will see that the Chamber of Commerce have complained that you are prepared to make the authorised refund by ordinary Drawback only, and ask that, for the reasons stated, the total amount to be refunded be issued in cash to the Chamber of Commerce for distribution among the individual merchants concerned, and to request you to submit a report on this matter.

I am to add that while the Inspector General

The Commissioner of Customs,

A I G U N.

General does not approve in principle of the suggestion that the total amount to be refunded should be handed over to the Chamber of Commerce for distribution, he considers that each exporter is, in the circumstances, entitled to a refund <u>in cash</u> of the amount of duty paid by him in respect of Flour exported during the period 1st April to 15th October during which period Flour was being passed free on export by the Harbin Customs. You are authorised, therefore, to make such refund in cash on the individual application of any of the said exporters, but no refund is to be made through the Chamber of Commerce without definite instructions authorising you to do so.

I am,

Sir,

Your obedient Servant,

Cecil A. V. Bowra

Chief Secretary.

<u>Appendix</u>.

Appendix.

I. G. despatch No. 92,617 to Aigun

税務處令第一七六八號

中華民國十一年十二月十四日

案據黑河商會會長丁官堂等來呈以愛琿關自本年四月一日起至十月十五日止所征麫粉出口稅銀業經令准發還復請由關將該項稅款發交商會轉發各商並瀝陳應行發還現款不得以存票抵還理由四端呈請鑒核飭遵等情前來本處查前項准予發還之麫粉稅款究竟可否由該關以現款發還並能否准照所請全交該商會轉給商人之處相應抄錄原呈令行總稅務司查議具復以憑核奪可也此令

附抄件

照錄黑河商會呈

民國十一年十二月十一日

呈為愛琿關應發還麫粉稅不與現款有心取巧希圖影射仰懇轉飭繳現以維商業事竊查愛琿關於本年四月一日起濫征麫粉出口稅曾經本會呈請取消奉鈞處第四六號批並抄發令稿內開愛琿關由本年四月一日起至十月十五日止所征麫粉出口稅銀概予發還麫商具領等因在案本會當以此項麫粉出口稅銀若由各商自行具領則手續層疊不惟與各商諸多不便即與愛琿關亦恐諸多煩瑣當即函請愛琿關將此項麫

粉出口稅銀查明若干概行發交本會再由本會傳知各商分別具領以期捷便而昭信重
去後旋准該關稅務司送交本會佈告一張內開爲布告事照得茲奉
總稅務司令開自本年四月一日至十月十五日按章所收運往外洋麪粉之稅本關一概
退還作爲特案以示海關之無歧視哈黑商民凡有此項退款之要求者應於自布告之日
始三月之內携帶稅票前來呈驗倘與報單相符本關即於呈驗之日始三星期之內按照
關平銀用存票發還該存票可在本關征稅科用作稅銀以抵進出口應納之稅或零星或
完數儘可自由等因奉此合亟布告俾衆週知此布等因查各處海關向例凡客商原貨出
口應發還稅銀海關往往用存票發還辦法在各商執此存票即可用作稅銀以抵進出口
應納之稅一舉兩便未爲不可然此不過爲原貨出口應退回之稅銀每月無幾家每家無
幾次爲此便利辦法本屬可行至此次該關所征之麪粉出口稅一違法濫征與原貨出口
退稅不同此必須發還現款者一也二行商散客除此項麪粉而外亦無他項買賣嗣後無
出口之貨無稅可納則存票無用此必須發還現款者二也三本鎮大商每趁開江時交通

便利往往運輸出口之貨足數封江後半年之用封江後即有運輸出口之貨亦寥寥無幾各商已納此項麪粉出口稅積至千數百元者有之或千餘元數百元者亦有之現距開江爲期六七個月出口之貨甚少應納之稅實已無多若以此千數百元或千餘元數百元之存票作抵稅款則爲日既久値此邊局擾亂尚不知有何變遷況黑河現在錢根奇緊各商受制發還此項鉅款地面亦可藉以通融且該關此次所徵麪粉出口稅爲時甚久爲數頗鉅倘不發還現款難免該麪商等不藉口與海關爲難倘一經衝突恐有意外情節此必須發還現款者三也四該關佈告內云自佈告之日始三月之內携帶稅票前來呈驗倘行商散客現不在黑三月之內不能携帶稅票呈驗試問此項稅銀該關歸公歟抑歸私歟難免不無影射況該關稅務司違法濫徵以病商邀功以禍國爲利此等貪橫

鈞處不從嚴懲辦以安邊商僅令將原款發還該關已不爲不幸乃更欲以違法亂徵之款與原貨出口退稅同一辦法實屬暗無天日此必須發還現款者四也以上四端均係正當理由並非格外要求本會代表衆商尤不能不爲之請命爲此備文呈請

鈞處鑒核轉飭愛琿海關稅務司將本年四月一日起至十月十五日止所徵麫粉出口稅銀查明開單連同現款一併送交本會轉發各商以期便捷而免弊混謹呈

趙桂山
趙學謙 同校

92.

I. G. Aigun / Taheiho 29th January, 23

Sir,

I have the honour to acknowledge the receipt of your despatch No. 102/92,617 :

calling for a report on the mode of refund of duty collected on flour exported abroad from 1st April to 15th October, 1922 ;

and in reply to inform you that on receipt of your despatch No. 88/91,787, enjoining refund of duty, I issued a Notification, which is enclosed, in english and chinese.

(Notification No. of 24th Nov. 1922

The following points require an explanation :

1. The <u>three months' limit</u> for presenting demands is justified by shortage of Staff : for the winter, I have the extra Clerk specially detailed for duty in connection with the collection of River Dues in summer. Hence my wish to despatch all the work, entailed by the refund of duties, before May. In the

summer

The Inspector General of Customs,

PEKING.

summer, the remainder of the Staff, already overcharged with work, could not be saddled with this extra job.

2. The <u>production of receipts</u> is an absolute necessity : much flour has been exported thorugh the Ferry Office, at which no application is ever made; the only trace of such payments and the only proof, is the Duty Receipt, and the butt filed with the Customs, on which however the name of the merchants is not given. - In case of flour exported through the General Office, the Duty receipt for which has been lost, I have allowed merchants to get duplicate receipts, provided they give accurate data on the original application.

3. I have issued <u>ordinary drawbacks</u> for one simple reason : I have no funds with which to pay cash drawbacks ; at the end of the year the balance in Revenue A/c. was Hk. Tls. 4,863.932, and in A/c. <u>A</u>, which for a large share is fed from Revenue funds, Hk.Tls. 335.01, while duties on flour, according to a summary calculation, amount to over Hk.Tls. 23,000. And, if cash must be paid to one, it must be paid to all.

4. The drawbacks can be presented for payment <u>only in the Taheiho General Office</u>, because there is a clerical Staff, competent with Indoor procedure, while at Aigun and at the Taheiho Ferry and Winter Road Office, there

are

are only Out-door Officers stationed. - But it is open to anybody to apply to the General Office for cargo to be passed through the Ferry Office or Winter Road Office, and that is what many merchants are doing.

That the present method works smoothly is proved by the following figures: up to 27th instant we have issued Drawbacks for Hk. Tls. 10,946.723 ; we have received another bunch of demands for Hk. Tls. 3,077.211 ; and duties for an amount of Hk. Tls. 5,915.927 have been paid by Drawback.

Coming now to the request of the Chamber of Commerce for refund of duties in a lump sum in cash, I have to say that, besides the usual reasons militating against such an extraordinary precedent, there is one point which is peremptory : a large share of the duties have been paid by Russians, another share, probably still larger, by travelling merchants, both of whom do not belong to the Chamber of Commerce (out of Hk.Tls. 10,946.723 issued, Hk.Tls. 3,090.913 have been issued to Russian merchants, while the amount issued to travelling merchants is hard to ascertain). There are besides several cases of flour exported through the Ferry Office, for which the duty receipt has been lost, and

and in many such cases the original exporter could not prove his identity to the Chamber, any better than to the Customs ; again, many travelling merchants have left town, and they are not likely to claim refund. So that the accusation of graft, more ridiculous than offensive when levelled at the Customs by the Chamber, can be retorted against the Chamber, whose aim in securing a lump sum can almost certainly be ascribed to the hope of pocketing the unclaimed sums.

In conclusion I must point out the insolent wording of the document submitted by the Chamber, as a further proof of my contention that, the more concessions we make to local merchants, the more aggressive becomes their attitude and style ; for such people, kindness and consideration from the superior Authorities are synonimous with weakness, which is to be taken advantage of. It is my firm opinion that the acceptance and transmission by the Shui Wu Ch'u of petitions compiled in such rude and venomous terms, is calculated to impair our dignity, and ultimately to render our position most difficult, if not untenable.

I have, etc.

G. Boezi

Acting Commissioner.

致瑷珲关第 88/91787 号令　　　　海关总税务司署（北京）1922 年 10 月 30 日

尊敬的瑷珲关税务司：

根据第 60 号呈：

"根据免税名单自 1922 年 4 月 1 日起废除的指示，瑷珲关自该日起，对出口国外的面粉征收税款，结果收到海关监督帮助大黑河商会提交的请愿，因为哈尔滨关依然允许面粉免税出口，所以要求瑷珲关应照哈尔滨关办法，允许免税出口，并将已征税银退还。"

奉总税务司之命，兹告知贵署自 1922 年 4 月 1 日起征收面粉出口税的行为正确无误。

很遗憾，因对指令有误解，哈尔滨关在 1922 年 4 月 1 日之后依然对面粉实行免税出口，其在收到贵署自行抄送给瑷珲关致海关总税务司第 60 号呈副本之前都未发现遗漏本项税款的征收。

由于与日本公使的现存协议，安东关铁路运输出口面粉应与北满洲铁路运输出口面粉采用相同的征税办法，故有必要将北满洲面粉征税办法上报中国政府。税务处最终规定，自 1922 年 10 月 16 日起，经北满洲境内海关出口的面粉与安东关铁路运输出口的面粉以同种办法征税。

从随附的税务处信函副本可知，瑷珲关关区面粉商人请求退还哈尔滨关面粉征税开始日期前在瑷珲关出口面粉所付的税银，并且商人请愿已予以批准。

贵署应将 1922 年 4 月 1 日至 10 月 15 日（包含这两日）期间所征税银退还。

您忠诚的仆人

包罗（C. A. Bowra）

总务科税务司

致瑷珲关第 102/92617 号令　　海关总税务司署(北京)1923 年 1 月 8 日

尊敬的瑷珲关税务司:

根据海关总税务司署第 88/91787 号令:

"瑷珲关自 1922 年 4 月 1 日至 10 月 15 日期间按章所征面粉(小麦)税款,一概退还。"

奉总税务司命令,兹附税务处第 1768 号令副本及其附件。据此令所示,黑河商会对贵署拟用存票发还税款表示了不满,并陈述了一些不宜按照常规办法进行退税的理由,要求贵署将全部税款以现款方式退还给商会,之后商会会将款项发还给各位商人。针对此事,总税务司要求贵署提交一份报告。

另外,总税务司虽然原则上不赞同将全部税款退还给商会、再由商会进行分发的建议,但对于此种情况,其认为既然自 4 月 1 日至 10 月 15 日哈尔滨关特批面粉出口免税放行,那么每位在此期间出口面粉的出口商都有资格获得现金返税。因此,授权贵署为个人申请退税的出口商退还税款,但是贵署在没有得到明确指示之前,不得将税款经由商会返回。

您忠诚的仆人

包罗(C. A. Bowra)

总务科税务司

呈海关总税务司署 92 号文　　瑷珲关 / 大黑河 1923 年 1 月 29 日

尊敬的海关总税务司（北京）：

根据海关总税务司署第 102/92617 号令：

“请汇报自 1922 年 4 月 1 日至 10 月 15 日期间对出口至国外的面粉所征关税的退税办法。”

兹报告，一经收到海关总税务司署第 88/91787 号令的退税指示，本署旋即发布汉英双语公告，随呈附上瑷珲关 1922 年 11 月 24 日第 24 号公告抄件。

关于此公告，需做出以下解释：

1. 关于限于三个月内提出退税申请事：瑷珲关人手不足，仅冬季会额外有一名供事专门负责夏季江捐税收的统计工作，因此本署希望可于五月前完成所有退税工作。入夏之后，剩余职员均是超负荷工作，难以承担此项额外工作。

2. 关于重新制作票据事：面粉大多经横江码头检查处出口至国外，但此处从未要求填写报单，交税的唯一记录及凭证仅有完税收据，以及海关存档的票根，然票根上亦从未登记过商人之姓名；此外，经征税汇办处出口之面粉，相关完税收据均已丢失。本署已向商人允诺，凡能提供原报单准确信息者，均可得收据的正副张。

3. 关于签发普通存票事：瑷珲关资金不足，无法支付兑现存票，截至 1922 年年底，税收账户仅余 4863.932 海关两，A 账户（主要由税收账户提供资金）仅余 335.01 海关两，而经粗略计算，面粉税收合计超过 23000 海关两。若出现以现款退税之例，则所有商人皆须以现款支付。

4. 关于仅可于大黑河征税汇办处提交存票抵付关税事：唯大黑河征税汇办处有一名供事可胜任内班事务，办理相关手续，瑷珲口岸和大黑河横江码头检查处及冬令过江检查处均只有外班关员驻守。但向征税汇办处申请货物自横江码头检查处或冬令过江检查处通过一事皆可，且多数商人均如此行事。

目前该退税办法进展顺利，截至 1923 年 1 月 27 日，已签发之退税存票金额共计 10946.723 海关两；随后又收到 3077.211 海关两之退税申请；目前已用存票抵付之关税共计 3915.927 海关两。

关于商会请求以现金一次性退税一事，且不说从未有过此等先例，仅从纳税之人的角度来看，此要求亦不甚合理，因为已收关税中，有很大一部分为俄国人交纳，更大一部分为行商交纳，而双方皆非商会成员（已签发之退税存票 10946.723 海关两中有 3090.913 海关两退予俄国商人，但退予行商之金额难以确定）。此外，通过横江码头检查处出口之面粉亦有遗失完税收据者，而此等面粉之原出口商既无法向海关证明身份，亦无法向商会证明；另有诸多行商已离开本埠，几无申请退税之可能。由此可见，商会所以提出以现金一次性退税之要求，确有中饱私囊之嫌，至于商会诬告海关欲私吞应退税款之事，更是荒谬至极。

商会提交之请愿书言辞粗鲁无礼，足以证明海关对当地商人越发妥协，越会招致其挑衅之态度；对此等人而言，政府之仁慈及体恤便为其可以利用之弱点。本署坚持认为，税务处接收并传达言辞粗鲁刻薄之请愿书有损海关尊严，若海关不能坚持立场，最终处境会十分不利。

您忠诚的仆人

包安济（G. Boezi）

瑷珲关署理税务司

7. 为戊通航业公司轮船装运之自用木柈免税放行事

SERVICE No. 45

No. 34. Service.

Aigun. No. 829.

CUSTOM HOUSE,

Harbin, 21st March, 1923.

Sir,

1. Enclosed please find copy of I. G. despatch to Harbin No. 2946/91,298 of 28th September, last.

Wood Fuel : for (Wu) T'ung Navigation Company's Steamers : to be passed free of duty : Instructions.

2. As wood fuel for steamer use is invariably passed free on the Sungari and Amur Rivers, I take it that the wood referred to is that shipped by the Company's steamers or barges in excess of their immediate requirements and/or landed at places controlled or uncontrolled by the Customs, for future use by other of the Company's steamers. As most steamers ship just sufficient for their immediate needs at points uncontrolled by the Customs, the quantities which, in compliance with the instructions of the above despatch, it will be necessary to exempt from duty are relatively small.

3. In addition to exempting, as before, all wood for steamers' immediate need, I propose to exempt from duty all excess quantities shipped at or passing Customs Stations on board steamers of the Wutung Co. up to the quantity of 40,000 Sajèn. Each of the Customs Stations in the Harbin District will, also, pass free of duty wood landed and declared to be for future shipment for steamer use.

4.

To

The Commissioner of Customs.

AIGUN.

4. Further I propose for each office in the Harbin District to keep a record of excess firewood shipped or carried by the Wutung Co. and passed free of duty, and of firewood landed free of duty and subsequently re-shipped for steamer use. Firewood landed but not re-shipped as above becomes dutiable.

5. In order to ensure that the annual maximum of 40,000 Sajèn is not exceeded, I have to request you to supply me with a monthly return on the above lines.

6. A copy of this despatch is being forwarded to the Inspector General.

I am,

Sir,

Your obedient Servant,

Nell d'Luque

Commissioner.

Shyp.

No. 2946 Commrs.

Harbin No. 91,298

INSPECTORATE GENERAL OF CUSTOMS,

PEKING, 28th September, 1922.

Sir,

I append, for your information and guidance, copy of Shui-wu Ch'u despatch No. 1245 and letter No 1311, from which you will see that, as a special favour, the Board has granted the request of the Mao T'ung Navigation Company (戊通航業公司) for duty-free treatment of wood used by its steamers for fuel, and that consequently you are to exempt such wood from duty up to a maximum of 40,000 沙繩 (Sajen ?) per year.

You are requested to act accordingly but in order to ensure that the above maximum is not exceeded you are to make an arrangement with the Aigun Office whereby the aggregate quantity passed by both your and that office is kept within this maximum.

I am,

Sir,

Your obedient Servant,

(signed) F. A. Aglen

Inspector General.

The Commissioner of Customs,

HARBIN.

[K.—21]

照錄稅務處來文

稅務處令第一二四五號中華民國十一年九月十三日

准財政部函稱准交通部咨開戊通航業公司本屬官商合辦年來虧累甚鉅為維持中國航權起見其自用木柴似應准予一律豁免稅捐以示體恤咨請核復等因查戊通航業公司之設原意係在挽救中國航權年來該公司既屬虧累其自用木柴似可准予豁免稅捐以示體恤而維航權應鈔錄原件函請查核見復以憑辦理等因前來查輪船自帶燃用煤斤均准免稅項此次戊通航業公司各輪船所用木柴亦係供作輪船燃料之用既據該公司聲稱年來營業虧累甚鉅應即通融准予免稅每年以四萬沙繩為限用示維持至木石局捐應由財政部轉飭一律豁免除函復並分令外相應抄錄原件令行總稅務司轉令濱江琿春愛琿等關稅務司遵照辦理此令附件

[K.—21]

照抄交通部咨

交通部為咨行事據戊通航業公司呈稱公司各輪船所用燃料係由沿江一帶自行裝運木柴此項木柴以俄國長度沙繩計算每年約需四萬沙繩之譜價值約二十餘萬元歷年海關暨木石税局均未徵税收捐自本年起海關忽釐定税率按每沙繩徵收税款洋三角年計四萬沙繩共應納海關税一萬餘元木石税局亦勒令繳税按每沙繩徵税六角之譜每年又需税款二萬餘元兩項税捐共計四萬餘元無論公司值賠累不堪之餘每年以二十餘萬元之鉅款購買燃料已屬困難萬分若再擔負税款數萬元實無力支持且公司係屬官商合辦部股占四分之三所營事業多關國政對於東三省所盡義務亦屬甚多如沿江軍隊調遣換防隨時使用公司輪船官廳人員因公往來乘船多送免票等而政府及三省官廳對於公司並無何種補助此項自用木柴並非販賣性質似應豁免一切捐税以資維持而重官業擬懇咨請財政部轉行税務處令飭哈爾濱江關並由財政部逕令吉黑兩省財政

[K.—21]

廳對於公司輪船裝運自用木柴一律豁免稅捐俾符向例等情前來
查該公司本屬官商合辦年來虧累甚鉅為維持中國航權起見其自
用木柴似應准予一律豁免稅捐以示體恤相應咨請
查照核辦見復以憑轉飭至紉公誼此咨
財政總長

署交通總長高恩洪

稅務處來函第一三二一號中華民國十一年九月二十五日

逕復者關於戊通航業公司輪船自用木柴准予免稅一事接展
來函內稱查木柴一項原在中俄陸路通商免稅物品之內但因前曾奉令取消
中俄條約之故濱江關對於此項木柴自本年四月一日起亦已照征稅款現在戊
通航業公司各輪所用之木柴已經鈞處決定通融免稅惟查海關對於輪船自
帶燃用之煤斤如所用係屬土煤向例均令照完出口正稅今鈞處准將該公司輪

[K.—21]

用木柴免征税款似以輪用煤斤之例為根據現按根據上既稍有不符所有此次令載木柴免稅一節是否仍應遵辦抑或另有變更之處理合函請鑒核酌定示復遵行等語本處查輪船自用土煤原係向完出口正稅則戊通公司輪船所用木柴如屬於土產者亦應按照土煤辦法辦理惟念該公司係官商合力創辦年來虧累甚鉅自不能不酌予維持且前項木柴每年免稅之數又以四萬沙繩為度限制尚嚴核與稅收亦無大碍所有該公司輪船自用木柴應即無論是否土產概行通融免稅俟將來該公司營業發達時再斟酌情形另議辦法相應函復

查照辦理專復順頌

公綏

-29]

0 COMMRS.

gun No.91,299

INSPECTORATE GENERAL OF CUSTOMS,

PEKING, 28th September, 1922.

Sir,

I append, for your information and guidance, copy of Shui-wu Ch'u despatch No. 1245 and letter No. 1311, from which you will see that, as a special favour, the Board has granted the request of the Mao T'ung Navigation Company (戊通航業公司) for duty-free treatment of wood used by its steamers for fuel, and that consequently you are to exempt such wood from duty up to a maximum of 40,000沙繩(Sajen ?) per year.

You are requested to act accordingly but in order to ensure that the above maximum is not exceeded you are to make an arrangement with the Harbin Office whereby the aggregate quantity passed by both your and that office is kept within this maximum.

I am,

Sir,

Your obedient Servant,

F. Aglen

Inspector General.

Commissioner of Customs,

AIGUN.

致瑷珲关第34/829号函　　　　　　　　　哈尔滨关1923年3月21日

尊敬的瑷珲关税务司:

1. 根据1922年9月28日海关总税务司署致哈尔滨关第2946/91298号令:

"凡戊通航业公司轮船自用木柈,皆免税放行。"

2. 在松花江及黑龙江,轮船自用木柈一直免税,兹说明:上述免税木柈乃指由戊通航业公司轮船或驳船运送者,超出该公司轮船即时所需之部分可运至受海关管控或不受海关管控各地,供该公司其他轮船今后使用。根据海关总税务司署相关指令,免税木柈之数量相对较少,故而多数轮船在无海关管辖各地仅装运供其即时所需之木柈。

3. 除一如往常对轮船即时所需之自用木柈免税外,兹提议:戊通航业公司轮船年度装载超限(除用作轮船燃料外)木柈总数未超过40000沙绳①时,在海关装运或途径海关时一律免税。哈尔滨关各分关亦将对着陆并申报今后为该公司其它轮船装运之木柈免税放行。

4. 此外,建议哈尔滨关各分关详细记录以下信息:戊通航业公司轮船超限(除用作轮船燃料外)装载或运输的免税木柈数量、免税着陆随后重新装船供该公司轮船使用之木柈数量。凡木柈着陆后未重新装船者,皆应纳税。

5. 为确保年度超限木柈数量不超过最高限额40000沙绳,请每月将上述记录以报表形式发送至本署。

6. 此函抄件将发送至海关总税务司署。

您忠诚的仆人

(签字)覃书(R. C. L. d' Anjou)

哈尔滨关税务司

① sajen是俄国的非公制长度单位,约合2.14米,中文有沙绳或俄丈两种译法。

哈尔滨关致瑷珲关第 34 号函附录

致哈尔滨关第 2946/91298 号令　　　　海关总税务司署（北京）1922 年 9 月 28 日

尊敬的哈尔滨关税务司：

兹附税务处第 1245 号令及 1311 号信函抄件，以供参考。从中可知，为以示体恤，税务处已批准戊通航业公司之申请，即凡该公司轮船用木柈燃料，皆免除关税，但哈尔滨关每年可予免税之木柈不得超过 40000 沙绳。

请遵照此命，但为确保免税木柈总量不超过此限额，请与瑷珲关一同作出安排，确保哈尔滨关及瑷珲关所免税放行之此等木柈数量不超过 40000 沙绳。

您忠诚的仆人

（签字）安格联（F. A. Aglen）

总税务司

致瑷珲关第80/91299号令　　　　海关总税务司署（北京）1922年9月28日

尊敬的瑷珲关税务司：

为了便于贵署顺利执行，兹附税务处第1245号令及第1311号函副本，以供参考。据此所示，税务处同意给予戊通航业公司特殊优待，对其公司轮船自用薪柴免税放行。故，贵署应对此类木料予以免税，且每年以40000沙绳为限。

敬请遵照此令执行，但为了确保每年免税数目不超过最人运输量，贵署应与哈尔滨关协商安排，让贵关与哈尔滨关过关总量处于上述限制范围之内。

您忠诚的仆人

安格联（Francis Arthur Aglen）

海关总税务司

8. 为呈送由满洲阿什河糖厂及其他工厂生产之块糖的征税办法事

[A.—39]

No. 138 COMMRS.

Aigun No. 95,009

INSPECTORATE GENERAL OF CUSTOMS,

PEKING, 6th July 1923.

Replied to ... 132.

Sir,

I am directed by the Inspector General to append hereto copy of a letter from the Ashiho Sugar Factory and Refinery Co., Ltd.:

> relating to the question of the duty treatment of lump sugar manufactured and exported by that Company;

and to request you to forward a report on the matter, with particular reference to the activities of this and other similar factories and the duty treatment of their products, especially lump sugar.

I am,

Sir,

Your obedient Servant,

(Signed)

Chief Secretary Officiating.

The Commissioner of Customs,

AIGUN.

Appendix.

Entered in Card-Index.

Appendix.

I. G. despatch No. 138/95,009 to Aigun.

Copy: Letter from Ashiho Sugar Factory & Refinery Co.,Ltd.to I.G.

Ashiho, June 14th, 1923.

Sir,

We have the honor to request you to explain to your Dairen Customs that the export duty on lump sugar of local origin according to the export tariff in force must be collected at the rate of Hk.Tls.0.200 per picul. Such measure of duty is levied by the Harbin, Manchuria and other Customs on such article. We have before us also official letters received from the Customs, under date of April 20/May 3,1915,No.158 and also June 6, 1923, No. 12, confirming the above fixed rate of duty.

The export tariff is precisely classified as follows :

Sugar Brown, /Nos.I to IO inclusive Dutch Stand/ 0.120
Sugar White, /Nos.II and upwards,incl.Dut. " / 0.200
In that way the highest duty on sugar is Hk.Tls. 0.200 per picul.

Allow me please to call your attention to the fact that lump sugar is a product of a large consumption just as well as the granulated sugar. Overcharging lump sugar with a high tariff, it may finally paralyse its production and without it, the activity of this Sugar Factory will

will be no doubt weaker, and the consequence will be the breaking down of the sugar-beet agriculture in Manchuria.

Applying a normal tariff duty on the lump sugar exported, the Customs will be benifitted with a much larger revenue than overcharging a high rate of duty on it, in the later case, the exportation of lump sugar will be completely paralized.

We may mention that instead of 425 shan of land sown with sugar beet last year, there are now already sown 4620 shan of beet this year and we hope to see that the output of sugar this season will be 200.000 poods of sugar instead of 4I.500 poods in last year.

It will be very unfortunate to see if the high duty be applied to the lump sugar, in such a case it will be a barrier against our export of this kind of sugar.

This will not be profitable to the Customs also, high tariff as that is against the fixed laws and no where such duty is applied except in Dairen.

We have the honor to request you that you will be so kind to send us a copy of your instructions that you will give to the Dairen Customs for our information.

We have the honor to be, etc.,

(Signed) M. Kassar,

Director.

copy:

[signature]

Acting Assistant Secretary.

SUGAR,LUMP: manufactured by Ashiho Sugar Factory and other factories in Manchuria: report on duty treatment of, submitting.

32.

.G.

Aigun 18th. August, 1923.

Sir,

1. I have the honour to acknowledge receipt of your Despatch No. 138:

SUGAR,LUMP:
Manufactured by Ashiho Sugar Factory
and other factories in Manchuria;
duty treatment of; report called for;

and, in reply, to state that there is little of interest that I can find to report on this subject.

2. The Ashiho Sugar Factory and Refinery CO., Ltd., opened an agency at Taheiho on the 8th. September, 1922, but the price at which their lump sugar was offered for sale - 25 cents a pound as compared with 20 cents a pound for Japanese lump sugar and 15 cents a pound for refined sugar from Hongkong, made it impossible for stocks to go satisfactorily into circulation, and the agency was closed on the 11th. February, 1923. Importations

from

The Inspector General of Customs,

Peking.

Entered in Card-Index.

from Harbin of lump sugar manufactured by the Ashiho Sugar Factory and Refinery Co., Ltd., amounted to Piculs 16.37 in 1922, and Piculs 2.70 have been imported so far this year. This sugar paid duty at Harbin at the rate of Hk.Tls. 0.2.0.0 a picul, no duty having been collected by this office. I should add that cargo imported by steamers consists of goods which have paid duty at one or other of the Sungari Custom Houses, and that River Dues only are collected here.

3. Refined Sugar, manufactured by the South Manchuria Sugar Factory of Moukden (南满製糖株式會社) and by the Hulan Sugar Manufacturing Company (呼蘭製糖廠), is offered for sale locally at 14 cents a pound, but business is done on a small scale only as people prefer to buy the superior and cleaner-looking article manufactured at Hongkong. Sugar manufactured at Moukden and Hulan also pays duty to the Harbin Customs at the rate of Hk.Tls. 0.2.0.0

per

per picul.

4. The prices at which various kinds of sugar are sold locally can be seen by reference to the following table:-

Local Sale Prices 1923.

	Picul. $	Pood. $	Pound. $
Lump Sugar:			
Ashiho	35.28	9.60	0.24
Japanese	29.40	8.00	0.20
Ashiho	27.20	7.50	0.18
Refined Sugar:			
Hongkong	22.05	6.00	0.15
Hulan	20.58	5.60	0.14
South Manchuria	20.58	5.60	0.14
Ashiho	18.38	5.00	0.12

5. There are three Flour Mills in this district - two at Taheiho and one at Aigun - but there are at present no other local manufactures or products.

I have the honour to be,

Sir,

Your obedient Servant,

R. F. C. Hedgeland

Commissioner.

致瑷珲关第 138/95009 号令　　　　海关总税务司署（北京）1923 年 7 月 6 日

尊敬的瑷珲关税务司：

奉总税务司命令，兹附阿什河制糖厂与精炼厂有限公司信函副本：

“关于该公司生产出口块糖的征税办法问题。”

请贵署呈送一份关于此问题的报告，尤其是要说明上述工厂及其他类似工厂的生产活动，及其产品（特别是块糖）的征税办法。

您忠诚的仆人

威厚澜（R. H. R. Wade）

代理总务科税务司

附件

阿什河制糖厂与精炼厂有限公司致海关总税务司署函　　1923年6月14日，阿什河

尊敬的海关总税务司：

烦请解释大连关的做法：根据现行有效的出口税则，凡土产块糖出口税，大连关均以每担0.200海关两来征收。在哈尔滨关、满洲及其他海关均有对以上糖类征税的办法。在此之前，我们公司还收到了海关公函（1915年4月20日/5月3日第158号函及1923年6月6日第12号函），证实出口税按以上固定税率征收。

出口税则严格按以下类别分类：

赤糖/荷兰标准一至十号/0.120

白糖/荷兰标准十号以上/0.200

按此方式，糖税最高为每担0.200海关两。

贵署必须了解到，与砂糖一样，块糖产品的消耗量也非常大。关税征收过高可能会导致块糖生产疲软，倘若不再生产块糖，制糖厂生意无疑会衰落，最终必会导致满洲甜菜农业崩溃。

对出口块糖征收正常的关税，会给海关带来更多税收。征收过高反而会导致块糖出口彻底瘫痪。

去年种植甜菜425垧，产糖41.500普特，而今年已增长至4620垧，有望产糖200.00普特。

倘若对块糖征收高额关税，势必阻碍我们出口该种糖类。

同时这种做法对海关来讲也没有益处，高额关税违背市场定律，且只有大连收取如此之高的关税。

请向我们寄送一份贵署给大连关下达的指令副本，以供我们参考。

此副本内容真实有效，特此证明。

谨呈。

（签字）卡萨（M.Kassar）

董事

确认人签字：

福贝士（A. H. Forbes）

代理总务科副税务司

呈海关总税务司署 132 号文　　　　瑷珲关 1923 年 8 月 18 日

尊敬的海关总税务司（北京）：

1. 根据海关总税务司署第 138 号令：

“块糖：请汇报由满洲阿什河糖厂及其他工厂所生产之块糖的征税办法。”

兹汇报，关于此事，可述之处不多。

2. 阿什河制糖厂与精炼厂有限公司曾于 1922 年 9 月 8 日在大黑河开设经销店，但此店块糖售价为每磅 25 分，相比日本每磅 20 分的块糖以及香港每磅 15 分的精制糖毫无价格优势，故已于 1923 年 2 月 11 日关闭。1922 年自哈尔滨进口的阿什河制糖厂与精炼厂有限公司生产的块糖总计 16.37 担，今年截至目前已进口 2.7 担。此等块糖在进口前均已于哈尔滨关交纳税款，税率为每担 0.200 海关两，瑷珲关从未予以征税。

另需补充一点，由轮船进口之货物中含已于松花江沿线税关交税者，本关仅征收江捐。

3. 南满制糖株式会社及呼兰制糖厂生产的精制糖于本埠之售价为每磅 14 分，然此精制糖生意规模较小，百姓更青睐香港所产外形精美之优质精制糖。奉天及呼兰生产的糖亦于进口前在哈尔滨关交纳税款，税率同为每担 0.200 海关两。

4. 各类糖于本埠之售价可参见下表：

	1923 年		
	担	普特	磅
块糖：	银圆	银圆	银圆
阿什河	35.28	9.60	0.24
日本	29.40	8.00	0.20
阿什河	27.20	7.50	0.18
精制糖：			
香港	22.05	6.00	0.15
呼兰	20.58	5.60	0.14
南满	20.58	5.60	0.14
阿什河	18.38	5.00	0.12

5. 此外，瑷珲关区共有三家面粉厂，其中两家位于大黑河，一家位于瑷珲，目前暂无其他本地制品。

您忠诚的仆人

贺智兰（R. F. C. Hedgeland）

瑷珲关税务司

9. 为汇报瑷珲关酒桶登记惯例事

Kerosene oil drums and other containers (C.3495): local practice re registration of Spirit Drums, reporting.

170.

I.G.

Aigun 7th. June, 1924.

Entered in Card-Index.

Sir,

1. I have the honour to acknowledge receipt of your Circular No. 3495:

> Kerosene oil drums and other containers: registration of, " pass-book system " for, size of drums, etc.; report called for;

and to submit the following reply.

2. The registration of Spirit Drums is effected at this port under the authority of I.G.Despatch No. 28/87,963. These drums are marked and numbered under Customs supervision, and when they have once paid duty, and have been engraved in a way that makes each drum easily identifiable, they are allowed to pass to and fro without further payment. A Register is kept in which is recorded the movement of each drum.

3.

The Inspector General of Customs,

Peking.

3. The " pass-book system " does not exist at this port.

4. The sizes of the various drums imported at this port are as follows:-

Length.	Diameter.	Capacity. (Gallons)
3'10"	2'11"	176.31
4'00"	2'9"	152.55
3'8"	2'8"	141.21
3'8"	2'8"	139.05
3'8"	2'6"	122.31
3'5"	2'6"	101.25

I have the honour to be,

Sir,

Your obedient Servant,

R. F. C. Hedgeland

Commissioner.

REFERENCES.

DESPATCHES.

From I.G. Commrs. No.	To I.G. Port No.
19/87,330	14
28/87,963	25

呈海关总税务司署 170 号文　　　　　　　　　　　　　瑷珲关 1924 年 6 月 7 日

尊敬的海关总税务司（北京）：

1. 根据海关总税务司署第 3495 号通令：

“煤油桶及其他容器：在‘派司簿’中登记容器尺寸等；请提交相关报告。”

兹报告如下：

2. 本口酒桶登记办法乃照海关总税务司署第 28/87963 号令指示办理。酒桶均须于海关的监督下进行标记及编号，凡已完纳一次关税者，均于桶身印刻易识别的标记，之后过关时则无须再次交税。酒桶去向均登记在册。

3. 本口尚未使用“派司簿”。

4. 进口至本口岸的各类桶尺寸如下：

长度	直径	容量（加仑）
3'10"	2'11"	176.31
4'00"	2'9"	152.55
3'8"	2'8"	141.21
3'8"	2'8"	139.05
3'8"	2'6"	122.31
3'5"	2'6"	101.25

您忠诚的仆人

贺智兰（R. F. C. Hedgeland）

瑷珲关税务司

10. 为奉令提交罐装油征税办法报告事

DUTY TREATMENT: CASE OIL: report on duty treatment accorded to, submitting.

186.

18. Aigun 1st. September, 24

Entered in Card-Index.

Sir,

I have the honour to acknowledge receipt of Circular No. 3540 :

> Duty treatment: case oil: report on duty treatment accorded to, called for;

and, in reply, to state that at this port duty on case oil is levied on the Tariff unit of 2 tins, each containing 5 American gallons.

I have the honour to be,

Sir,

Your obedient Servant,

R. F. C. Hengeler

Commissioner.

The Inspector General of Customs,

Peking.

呈海关总税务司署 186 号文　　瑷珲关 1924 年 9 月 1 日

尊敬的海关总税务司（北京）：

根据海关总税务司署第 3540 号通令：

"征税办法：请汇报罐装油征税办法。"

兹报告，瑷珲关罐装油关税按每 2 罐为 1 个征税单位征收，每罐装有 5（美）加仑。

您忠诚的仆人

贺智兰（R. F. C. Hedgeland）

瑷珲关税务司

11. 为自 1930 年 1 月 20 日起减征豆油出口正税及免征豆饼出口附加税之指示事

COMMRS. No. 125,784

Aigun No. 511

No.

SHANGHAI OFFICE OF THE
INSPECTORATE GENERAL OF CUSTOMS, 22nd January, 1930.

SIR,

I append, for your information and guidance, copy of Kuan-wu Shu despatch No. 1,847, from which you will see that in order to give relief to the Manchurian trade in bean products, the Government has ruled that all Manchurian bean-oil and bean-cake exported abroad are to be exempted from payment of Export Surtax, while the export duty on bean-oil is to be reduced from three mace to two mace a picul to take effect at all Customs in Manchuria beginning from the 20th January, 1930.

You are requested to act accordingly.

A telegram to this effect was sent to your address on the 19th January.

I am,

Sir,

Your obedient Servant,

Inspector General.

Appendix.

The Commissioner of Customs,

AIGUN.

财政部關務署令第一八四七號 中華民國十九年壹月十三日

令總稅務司梅樂和

爲令行事案准

行政院秘書處函以工商部提議擬准哈爾濱東北油坊同業聯合會所請將大豆出口稅增加油餅出口稅免除事議案經提出第四十八次院議決議交財政工商兩部於會議新關稅稅則時參酌擬訂等因函達查照到部當經發交國定稅則委員會辦理茲據該會將會議情形呈報前來查大豆加稅應如該會所議仍於修訂出口稅則時並案辦理以臻妥適所有油餅出口稅如予完全免除則其他出口之油類餅類亦應俱免方昭公允以此事涉既多影響稅收過鉅惟東北油類事業近年相繼停歇困苦確係實情應將所征稅項特予分別減免俾資救濟茲經規定凡屬東三省所產豆油豆餅於輸出外洋時概予免征二五出口附稅其豆油一項原征出口正稅爲

每擔關平銀三錢亦予改按每擔關平銀二錢征收出口稅即由部令飭東三省各海關自本年一月二十日起一律實行俾於體恤商艱之中圖庫不致影響通籌面推行既以灌利該商亦得藉以維持至東三省所征各項豆油捐當地稅捐並應由東三省酌量減免以示格外維持之意除已由部呈復

行政院鑒核咨行東北政務委員會查照辦理並令行東三省各海關監督遵照外合行令仰遵照迅即通令東三省各海關稅務司自本年一月二十日起照部定減免辦法辦理爲要此令

文牘員 周歐明 校

致瑷珲关第511/125784号令　　　　海关总税务司署(上海),1930年1月22日

尊敬的瑷珲关税务司：

为了便于贵署顺利执行，兹附关务署第1847号令副本，以供参考。据该令所示，为促进满洲豆制品贸易，政府规定，满洲所有海关自1930年1月20日起，凡出口境外的满洲豆油及豆饼，免除出口附加税，豆油出口正税从每担三钱减为每担两钱。

敬请遵照此令执行。

关于税金减免的电报已于1月19日发送至瑷珲关。

您忠诚的仆人

梅乐和（F. W. Maze）

总务科税务司

12. 为保税油罐及货仓的相关费用之指示事

COMMRS. No. 128,128

Aigun No. 536

No.

SHANGHAI OFFICE OF THE

INSPECTORATE GENERAL OF CUSTOMS, 24th May, 1930.

SIR,

With reference to I.G. despatch No. **529/127,443:**

Kerosene Oil, etc.: temporary facilities for bonding and shipment in bond granted to; instructions;

I am directed by the Inspector General to say that the initial fee of Hk. Tls. 250.00 and the annual fee of Hk. Tls. 50.00 as laid down in the Provisional Regulations appended to the above despatch, cover all tanks and warehouses in any one installation. The Supervision Fees under headings 3 and 4 are likewise to be read in the above sense.

I am,

Sir,

Your obedient Servant,

Chief Secretary.

issioner of Customs,

A I G U N.

致瑷珲关第 536/128128 号令　　　　　　海关总税务司署（上海）1930 年 5 月 24 日

尊敬的瑷珲关税务司：

根据海关总税务司署第 529/127443 号令：

“煤油等货物：批准建立临时关栈；相关指示。”

奉总税务司命令，兹通知，随上述令文所附的《临时章程》中规定申请许可的费用为 250.00 海关两及许可年度续期费用为 50.00 海关两，上述费用涵盖了油罐、货仓及其他所有装置。《临时章程》中第 3 项和第 4 项的监察费亦可参照上述理解。

您忠诚的仆人

华善（P. R. Walsham）

总务科税务司

13. 为批准放宽满洲港口出口谷物禁令事

COMMRS. No. 133,946

Aigun No. 590

No.

SHANGHAI OFFICE OF THE
INSPECTORATE GENERAL OF CUSTOMS, 31st March, 1931.

SIR,

I append, for your information and guidance, copy of Kuan-wu Shu despatches Nos. 2,649 and 4,558, from which you will see that, at the request of the Provincial Authorities, the Government has authorised the relaxing of the embargo on the exportation abroad of cereals, including rice, from Manchurian ports.

You are requested to act accordingly.

I am,
Sir,
Your obedient Servant,

Inspector General.

Appendix.

[Com]missioner of Customs,
A I G U N.

財政部關務署訓令第二六四九號　中華民國十九年五月十四日

令總稅務司梅樂和

爲令遵事奉

部長發下

國民政府訓令內開前據東北政務委員會張主席學良馬電據吉林省政府轉濱江市政籌備處請示可否准弛米禁等情業經送由　中央政治會議決議核復准其特別弛禁並經報告本府第七十二次國務會議查照辦理電復飭知去後茲據徑電稱據山海關監督洪維國電稱前奉中央令飭查禁奸商私運糧食出洋遵即轉行稅務司照辦茲據日商報由營口用輪裝運小米前往日本稅務司遵令不准出口駐營日領來署面稱前清宣統元年部處咨准東三省總督與日使商定東省所產小麥高糧包穀及粟豐年准由南滿海運出洋倘因外運過多民食缺乏先一個月知照屆期禁運根據成案聲請弛禁

前來查與成案相符東省上年豐稔本年春雨霑足民食不虞缺乏日商報運小米等項似應援照成案准予出洋可否之處懇乞示遵等情查東省民食現在不虞缺乏自係實情且上年產糧甚豐地方正患現貨缺少如果禁運出洋殊與國際民生大有關碍應請鈞府准予弛禁令行財政部轉飭海關遵照辦理將來遇有民食不足應行禁運之時自當先期呈請核准一面知照日使以免藉口特電奉達敬候示遵等情據此復經提出本府第七十四次國務會議決議照准在案除電知外合行抄發馬電及中央政治會議復函令仰該部查照併案轉飭遵照等因並附到鈔電及函各一件奉此除由部呈復並分行外合行令仰該總稅務司遵照此令

文郁
周敢明同校

財政部關務署訓令政字第四五五八號　中華民國二十年二月二十五日

令總稅務司梅樂和

爲令遵事奉

部長發下

行政院訓令以奉

國民政府交辦東北政務委員會呈據遼寧省政府呈請解除米禁一案查遼

省既有特別情形且吉林省前經

中央政治會議核准有案所請弛放遼省米禁自應照准合行令仰該部轉飭

遵照辦理等因除由部令行東北各海關監督轉飭各該關稅務司遵辦外合

行令仰該總稅務司遵照此令

文郁
蕭鍾祥　同校

致瑷珲关第590/133946号令　　　　海关总税务司署（上海），1931年3月31日

尊敬的瑷珲关税务司：

为了便于贵署顺利执行，兹附关务署第2649号令及第4558号令副本，以供参考。据该令所示，应省政府要求，政府已批准放宽满洲港口出口谷物（包括水稻在内的）禁令。

请遵照此令执行。

您忠诚的仆人

梅乐和（F. W. Maze）

海关总税务司

14. 为告知已批准对某些公司进口之卷烟施行临时赊税办法事

[A.—29]

COMMRS. No. 135,381

Aigun No. 605

No.

SHANGHAI OFFICE OF THE INSPECTORATE GENERAL OF CUSTOMS, 17th June, 1931.

INDEXED

SIR,

With reference to Circular No. 4224:

Consolidated tax on cotton yarn, cement, matches, rolled tobacco, and wheat flour; collection of, to be entrusted to Customs from 16th May, 1931, on all such goods imported from abroad or from provinces where consolidated tax is not in force; I.G.'s instructions re procedure to be adopted by Customs;

I am directed by the Inspector General to inform you that the Ministry of Finance has temporarily authorised a special system of credit for settlement of tax on rolled tobacco imported by certain firms whose names are given on the appended list.

In such cases, therefore, the procedure laid down in Section II of the Regulations appended to the above Circular is to be modified as follows. The merchant, after obtaining the yellow application and Consolidated Tax Memo. from the Customs (vide Section II § 3), will take these documents to the Bureau where they will be chopped " Release on credit;" he will then present the Consolidated Tax Memo. to the Customs Bank in the ordinary way, which will retain one section of the Memo., although no collection is made; on receipt of the remaining parts of the Tax Memo. bearing the above chop, the

The Commissioner of Customs,

A I G U N.

the Customs are to treat the goods as Tax-paid and release them accordingly.

Tax settled on this credit basis will be paid by the firms direct to the Consolidated Tax Administration at the end of each month and is not to be included in the Customs reports of collection. A footnote, however, is to be added to the monthly report (vide Enclosure No. 4 of above Circular) stating the amount of tax due each month on Rolled Tobacco released on credit.

This special credit procedure is to be observed as long as tax on Rolled Tobacco is collected in silver according to the Consolidated Tax Tariff.

I am,

Sir,

Your obedient Servant,

Chief Secretary.

Appendix.

FIRMS FOR WHOM SPECIAL CREDIT SYSTEM HAS BEEN AUTHORISED AND SHANGHAI ADDRESS OF EACH.

Establishment Boy Landry, 708-710 Avenue Joffre.

Holdo Stromwall, 17 Yuen Ming Yuen Road.

British American Tobacco Co., Ltd., 6 Soochow Road.

Liggett & Myers Tobacco Co., 2a Kiukiang Road.

United Kingdom Tobacco Co., 212 Szechuen Road.

Ardath Tobacco Co., 467 Kiangse Road.

致瑷珲关第605/135381号令　　　　海关总税务司署（上海），1931年6月17日

尊敬的瑷珲关税务司：

根据海关总税务司署第4224号通令：

"自1931年5月16日起，凡棉纱、水泥、火柴、卷烟及麦粉自不征收统税之外国或省份进口者，其统税皆由海关负责征收；于此，各关务必遵行海关总税务司署相关指令。"

奉总税务司命令，现批复如下：财政部已批准对某些公司进口之卷烟施行临时赊税办法，公司名称参见所附清单。

因此，海关总税务司署第4224号通令所附章程第二节将改为：商人自海关取得黄色报单及统税缴纳证后（参阅第二节 §3），先交由统税局加盖"赊税放行（release on credit）"印章，再照常将统税缴纳证送交海关银行，银行虽不收税，但会留存一联统税缴纳证，最后再将剩余加盖"赊税放行"印章的统税缴纳证送交海关，海关收到后将按完税货物予以放行。

赊欠之税款由相关公司于每月末直接缴纳至统税局，此外，无须将此等税款载入海关税收报告，但须在月报内添加脚注（参阅第4224号通令附件4），说明每月赊税放行卷烟的应税总额。

只要卷烟税仍照统税税则以银两进行征收，此项特殊赊税办法便不会被取缔。

您忠诚的仆人

岸本广吉（H. Kishimoto）

总务科税务司

附录

授权特殊赊税办法之公司及其位于上海之地址

公司名称[①]	地址
芭兰公司(Establissements Boy Landry)	霞飞路 708-710
瑞丰洋行(Holdo Stromwall)	圆明园路 17 号
英美烟草公司(British American Tobacco Co., Ltd.)	苏州路 6 号
大美烟公司(Liggett&Myers Tobacco Co.)	九江路 2a
金城烟公司(United Kingdom Tobacco Co.)	四川路 212
雅达烟公司(Ardath Tobacco Co.)	江西路 467

① 列表中除英美烟草公司(British American Tobacco Co., Ltd.)外,汉译名均查自孙修福先生所编《近代中国华洋机构译名大全》。

15. 为要求对所有进口糖品详细记录及汇报进口糖品征税情形事

[A.—29]

COMMRS. No. 140,827

Aigun No. 655

No.

SHANGHAI OFFICE OF THE
INSPECTORATE GENERAL OF CUSTOMS, 7th May, 1932.

SIR,

With reference to Circular No. 4404:
instructing that the polarisation system of classifying sugar is to be enforced from the 1st April and communicating a set of revised duty rates for sugar to be applicable from the same date;

and to I.G.'s confidential telegram of the 3rd April:
enumerating the steps to be taken with regard to enforcing the revised duty rates;

I append, for your information and guidance, copy of Kuan-wu Shu despatch No. 192 from which you will see that on my transmitting the Dairen Commissioner's report that, owing to the opposition of the Kwantung Government, he has not been able to enforce the new duty rates and is continuing to pass sugar on payment of duty at the old rates, the Shu state that although certain of the Customs in Manchuria may, on account of practical difficulties, have been unable to enforce the revised duty rates on sugar at the same time as other ports, the Government have not abandoned their right to collect duty at these revised rates, and that such Customs are therefore at some future date to claim from the merchants concerned the amount short-paid on any

importations

The Commissioner of Customs,

A I G U N.

importations of sugar which should have paid duty at the new rates. The Shu furthermore call for a report on the present position at the different ports in Manchuria with regard to the collection of duty on foreign sugar.

I have therefore to request you to act accordingly and to submit a report, with Chinese version in duplicate, describing your present practice in this connection. Should you have been unable so far to enforce the collection of duty on sugar at the revised rates, you are to note that a careful record of all sugar importations is to be kept so that a claim for any amounts short-paid may be made at some future date.

I am,

Sir,

Your obedient Servant,

Inspector General.

財政部關務署指令關字第一九二號　中華民國二十一年四月二十八日

令總稅務司梅樂和

呈一件大連關對於進口糖品改訂稅率一案未能如期實行請鑒核由

呈悉查進口糖品改按新訂稅率徵稅一事東省各關雖以事實上之困難未能同時實行惟政府並未放棄徵稅之權對於應徵新稅之糖品將來各關仍須按照短徵稅額向商人追繳據報關東廳以東省各口未實行糖品新稅之故遂謂大連關應徵糖貨新稅亦須緩行徵收理由至欠充分該關稅務司辦理此事最少限度應保留向商人追繳稅款之權對於進口糖品並應詳爲記錄以便將來照額追繳仰卽遵照辦理並將東省其他各關辦理糖稅情形具報查核爲要此令

黃晏民
張哲生　同校

致瑷珲关第655/140827号令　　　　海关总税务司署（上海），1932年5月7日

尊敬的瑷珲关税务司：

根据海关总税务司署第4404号通令：

“为自4月1日起实行糖品最新归类办法及进口糖品按照改订税率征税事。”

及海关总税务司署4月3日密电：

“详述改订税率征收办法。”

兹附关务署第192号训令，以供参考。从中可知，在收悉由本总税务司传达之大连关税务司关于伪满政府反对而未能实行改订税率，仍按旧税率对糖品征税一事之报告后，关务署表示，对于进口糖品改按新订税率征税一事，东省各关虽因实际困难未能与其他各关同时实行，但政府并未禁止此项征税，对于应征新税之进口糖品，将来各关仍须按照短缴税额向商人追缴，并要求东省各关汇报进口糖品征税情形。

请遵照办理，并呈交瑷珲关糖品现行征税办法报告，附汉文译本，一式两份。贵署目前若无法实行改订税率，则应对所有进口糖品详细记录，以便将来照额追缴。

您忠诚的仆人

梅乐和（F. W. Maze）